HISTORY OF THE BOMBAY AND KARNATAKA: MUSALMAN AND MARATHA (1300-1818)

HISTORY OF THE BOMBAY AND KARNATAKA: MUSALMAN AND MARATHA (1300-1818)

E. W. WEST

GYAN

Published by

GYAN

Gyan Publishing House
5, Ansari Road
Daryaganj, New Delhi-110002
Phone: 011-47034999, 9811692060
E-mail: books@gyanbooks.com

Distribution Network
gyanbooks.com
India, USA, Canada, UK, Australia, France

ISBN : 978-81-212-3537-2 (PB)
First Published, 1877

2nd Impression 2020

Printed at: Gyan Press, Delhi.

History of the
Bombay and Karnataka:
Musalman and Maratha
(1300-1818)
Author: E. W. West

HISTORY OF THE

BOMBAY KARNATAKA

HISTORY OF THE

BOMBAY KARNATAKA

MUSALMÁN AND MARÁTHA

A.D. 1300-1818

E.W. WEST

ASIAN EDUCATIONAL SERVICES
NEW DELHI ★ MADRAS ★ 1989

ASIAN EDUCATIONAL SERVICES.
* C-2/15, S.D.A. NEW DELHI-110016
* 5 SRIPURAM FIRST STREET, MADRAS-600014.

Price: Rs. 30
AES REprint: 1989
First Published: 1877
ISBN: 81-206-0468-9

Published by J. Jetley
for ASIAN EDUCATIONAL SERVICES
C-2/15, SDA New Delhi-110016
Processed by APEX PUBLICATION SERVICES
New Delhi-110 016
Printed at AGARWAL PRINTERS DELHI

HISTORY

OF THE

BOMBAY KARNATAK:

MUSALMÁN AND MARÁTHA,

A.D. 1300 - 1818.

BY THE LATE

MAJOR E. W. WEST,

JOINT ADMINISTRATOR OF SÁNGLI,

1878.

[*CONTRIBUTED 1877.*]

HISTORY OF THE BOMBAY KARNÁTAK.

MUSALMA'N AND MARA'THA (A.D. 1300-1818).

Historical Sketch of the Southern Mara'tha Country or Bombay Karna'tak, that is the territory included in the districts of Belgaum, Dha'rwa'r, and Bija'pur, from the Musalma'n Conquest till it became British territory: A.D. 1300-1818.

HISTORICAL SKETCH, A.D. 1300-1818.

Musalman Conquests.

THE raid into the southern part of the Peninsula made by Káfúr and the various Musalmán leaders who followed him (A.D. 1310-1327), effectually broke up the existing Hindu dynasties. To effect the conquest of the country thus overrun, more was required than isolated expeditions, and as each wave of invasion retired the Hindus seem to have made head again. The Pálegár chiefs regained their fortresses, and new dynasties replaced those which had been subverted. In considerably less than half a century after the Bellál rájás had been overthrown, new Hindu kingdoms were formed in the south, which for many a day were destined to be thorns in the sides of the Musalmáns. One leading kingdom was founded by an officer formerly in the service of the Bellál kings, at Vijayanagar on the Tungbhadra river opposite to Anigundi, which had been the capital of a more ancient but less important principality. Within the limits of the new kingdom was included the whole of the Southern Marátha Country as far north as Belgaum; the district immediately to the north of the last-named place being evidently in the hands of the Musalmáns, as Farishtah mentions an Amir of Hukeri. From this and other territorial titles incidentally referred to, we gather that in A.D. 1347, when the Bahamani dynasty was founded the districts of Bijápur Athni and Chikodi, in the tract of country which is the subject of the present sketch, formed part of its dominions.[1] The Musalmáns were by no means complete masters of all the country nominally subject to them. The effect of the terrible famine known as the Durga Devi, which began in A.D. 1396 and lasted twelve years, was to throw into the hands of pálegárs and robbers many strongholds previously conquered by the Muhammadans,[2] and so late as the reign of Máhmúd Sháh Bahamani II. (A.D. 1493), we read of a Hindu zamindár at Miraj.[3]

Vijayanagar.

The Bahámanis, A.D. 1347.

From an early period the Bahamani kings devoted their principal attention to attacks on Vijayanagar; but from Golkonda or Bidar as a base of operations, it was easier to overrun the districts of Raichur

---

[1] See an Historical Account of the Belgaum District by H. Stokes Esq. Madras C.S. Selections from the Records of the Government of Bombay, New Series, CXV. 12.

[2] Grant Duff's Maráthás, I. 43 (Indian Reprint).

[3] Briggs' Farishtah, III. 316.

HISTORICAL SKETCH, A.D. 1300-1818.

The Bahamanis attack the Southern Marátha Country.

and Mudgal, which lay between the two capitals, than to attempt the conquest of a tract like the Bombay Karnátak or Southern Marátha Country, less conveniently situated, and which is described by the Musalmán historian as full of fastnesses and woods, almost impenetrable to troops.[1] When the Muhammadans, after repeatedly taking and losing the forts of Raichur and Mudgal, at last established themselves in the districts commanded by these forts, they, after being baffled by the strength of the fortress of Adoni or Adwáni, turned their attention to the Southern Marátha Country, which their new conquests gave them the means of attacking from the south-east. In 1406 Firoz Sháh, the grandson of Alla-ud-dín Bahamani, besieged and took Bankápur, described by Farishtah as the most important fortress in the Karnátak; and this success placed at his mercy the southern part of what is now the Dhárwár collectorate. From Bankápur the Musalmáns gradually extended their arms in a northerly direction, though they seem to have advanced but slowly. Fifty years later Navalgund is mentioned as the seat of a *sarkár* or province; and it was there that Jalál Khán, governor of the province and brother-in-law of Ala-ud-dín Bahamani II., raised the standard of revolt (A.D. 1454) in the hope of seating his son Sikandar Khán on the throne, a step which led to the death of his son and his own imprisonment for life.

Take Bankápur, A.D. 1406.

Navalgund.

One of the chief leaders in the campaign against Jalál Khán was Máhmúd Gawán, who held the office of prime minister as well as the government of Bijápur. This able man distinguished himself highly in the reigns of Alla-ud-dín II. and Humáyún Shah Bahamani, but the greatest of his exploits was reserved for the reign of Muhammad Sháh II. In the historical sketch of Kolhápur an account is given of Máhmúd Gawán's campaign in Kolhápur and Vishálgad; after which he proceeded to attack the maritime possessions of the rája of Vijayanagar, and with such success that he took Goa in A.D. 1470. This led to the siege and capture of Belgaum; for, at the instigation of the Vijayanagar king Birkána Ray, that is Vikram Ray, rája of the fortress of Belgaum, marched or sent troops in 1472, together with the Hindu chief of Bankápur, to retake Goa. On this Muhammad Sháh collected his forces and moved against Belgaum, "a fortress of great strength, surrounded by a deep wet ditch, and near it a pass, the only approach to which was fortified by redoubts."[2] According to the Musalmán historian, Birkana Ray, who commanded the fort in person, at first asked for terms, which were refused. The Hindu chief then defended himself with great vigour, and effectually prevented the enemy from filling the wet ditch, in which lay the principal strength of the fort. The besiegers on this changed their tactics and tried the effect of mining, a mode of operation not hitherto used in the Dakhan. The new plan proved successful, three mines being sprung which made practicable breaches: these were immediately stormed; and notwithstanding the gallant defence made by the garrison and the severe

And Belgaum, A.D. 1472.

[1] Briggs' Farishtah, II. 337.

[2] Briggs' Farishtah, II. 491. The account in the text of the siege of Belgaum is taken from this historian.

HISTORICAL SKETCH, A.D. 1300-1818.

The Bahamanis, A.D. 1347-1489.

losses inflicted on the besiegers, the latter succeeded in gaining the ramparts. The inner citadel had yet to be carried, but Birkana Ray, despairing of being able to offer an effectual resistance, disguised himself and was admitted to the presence of the king as a messenger from the Hindu chief. He then drew the rim of his turban round his neck and discovered himself, saying that he had come with his family to kiss the foot of the throne. The king, pleased with this exhibition of confidence, admitted him into the order of nobility.

Famine of A.D. 1472.

The capture of Belgaum and the conquest of its dependencies brought the whole of the Southern Marátha Country under the Musalmáns, and for the time completely crushed the efforts of Hindu independence. The acquisitions were added to the estates of Khwája Máhmúd Gawán, who had taken a prominent part in the siege. Subsequently they were transferred by the minister to Fakhr-ul-Mulk.[1] In the year of the capture of Belgaum (A.D. 1472) and in the following year, a drought led to a terrible famine. No rain fell for two years; and, to use Farishtah's words: "The towns became almost depopulated; many of the inhabitants died of famine; and numbers emigrated for food to Málwa, Jájnagar in Katak, and Gujarát. In Telingana, Marhut that is Mahárashtra, and throughout the Bahamani dominions, no grain was sown for two years; and in the third, when the Almighty showered his mercy upon the earth, scarcely any farmer remained in the country to cultivate the land."[2]

Decline of the Bahamanis, A.D. 1481.

The unjust execution of the prime minister in A.D. 1481 on a false charge of treason precipitated the fall of the Bahamani dynasty. The great chiefs placed in charge of provinces had for some time been strengthening their own power at the expense of their sovereign, but as long as Máhmúd Gawán lived they were kept in check: his death relieved them from all restraints, and before long the chief provinces of the Bahamani kings became separate kingdoms. Of these the present sketch deals with Bijápur alone, which Yúsuf A'dil Khán Savái carved into a kingdom.

Yúsuf A'dil Khán.

Yúsuf A'dil Khán, who, after he had achieved greatness was declared to have been born to greatness,[3] had entered the service of the Bahamani king Máhmúd Sháh II., and had risen from rank to rank till he was made governor of the province of Daulatábád, a post which he held at the time of the minister's death. Immediately after that event the king sent for Yúsuf A'dil Khán, being compelled to do so by the attitude assumed by the other chiefs, and conferred on him the

---

[1] This leader was placed in charge of one of the eight provinces into which the prime minister at this time divided the Bahamani kingdom. His charge was "a tract from Junnar, including several dependent districts in the south, such as Indápur Wái and Mán, as well as the forts of Goa and Belgaum." The province of Bijápur was reserved by the minister for himself. Farishtah, II. 502.

[2] Briggs' Farishtah, II. 493.

[3] He was said to be a son of an emperor of Rúm (Turkey). After his father's death his brother, on succeeding to the throne, thought it would save future trouble if possible claimants were put out of the way. He accordingly demanded the child Yúsuf from his mother for execution. The mother managed to substitute a slave boy, who was strangled, and sent her son to Persia, whence he made his way to India. See Briggs' Farishtah, III. 4-8.

HISTORICAL SKETCH, A.D. 1300 - 1818.

Yúsuf declares himself King of Bijápur, A.D. 1489.

province of Bijápur. This and the other provinces seem to have been bestowed under pressure; and the leaders, who in this way gained power and place retained but a slender tie of allegiance to the sovereign to whose weakness and not to whose favour they were indebted. The Bahamani kingdom was distracted by the rivalry between the Dakhanis or born subjects, and the foreigners, who had introduced themselves in great numbers: and Yúsuf A'dil Khán was the leader of the latter party. It is needless to recapitulate the details of the struggles of the opposing parties. Ere long Yúsuf A'dil Khán followed the example of Malik Ahmad Beheri, who had declared himself king of Ahmadnagar, by having the public prayer read in his own name as king of Bijápur (A.D. 1489) and by assuming the canopy of royalty. He soon drove out the royal garrisons that were in the forts in his district and made himself complete master of the territory under Bijápur. Notwithstanding this he appears for some time to have kept up friendly relations with his former sovereign. He assisted Máhmúd Sháh to put down the rebellion of Bahádur Giláni, and afterwards entertained him royally at Bijápur.[1] He subsequently joined Máhmúd Sháh in his expedition against Kásim Barid, another chief who had assumed sovereignty; and it is especially noted that after the victory obtained on this occasion the king treated his former vassal as an equal, and made Yúsuf sit in his presence. The alliance was further cemented by the betrothal of Yúsuf's daughter to Ahmad, the king's son. Some years later Máhmúd Sháh got up a league against the Bijápur prince, the ostensible ground of action being that the latter had not only revolted against his sovereign but had also introduced Shia tenets into the country. The confederation failed to secure their object, and by their defeat Yúsuf A'dil Khán was able to establish his kingdom on a secure basis.[2]

The Limits of Bijápur.

The new dynasty succeeded to the southern territory of the Bahamani monarchy, but at first the limits of their dominions were more circumscribed than those of their predecessors, as, during the feeble sway and troubled reigns of the later Bahamani kings, the Vijayanagar rájás had recovered much of the country of which they had been dispossessed. In the reign of Yúsuf's son, Ismail A'dil Sháh, we find that Kittur was apparently the most southerly position occupied by the Musalmáns, Dhárwár having fallen into the hands of the Hindus, who had also possession of Torgal, so that the eastern and southern parts of the Southern Marátha Country had reverted to their old rulers. Afterwards the Bijápur kingdom extended from the Níra on the north to the Tungbhadra on the south, and from the

---

[1] Farishtah mentions at this period that Bijápur (apparently the fort) had recently been surrounded with a stone wall. When narrating the rebellion against Humáyún Sháh Bahamani that had taken place some thirty years previously (II. 467), he particularly noted that the fort was then (A.D. 1459) only built of mud. The stone wall round the city does not appear to have been finished till A.D. 1566. See Farishtah, III. 14 and 132.

[2] Yúsuf assumed and his successors retained the title of Sháh. The dynasty however was generally known by the title of A'dil Khán, which the old European travellers turned into Idalcam, Idalcan, and Dialkan. See Purchas's Pilgrimage and Van Linschoten's Travels.

HISTORICAL SKETCH, A.D. 1300-181

sea on the west to the Bhíma and Krishna on the east.[1] Later on its victorious arms were carried beyond the Tungbhadra, and to the south-east as far as the Bay of Bengal; and it is interesting to note that the Bijápur kings were brought in contact with two European nations destined to play a prominent part in Southern India. Thus Goa was taken from them on the west coast by Albuquerque, the Portuguese general, in A.D. 1510; while on the other side of the peninsula the French, in A.D. 1674, obtained a grant of the site of Pondicherry from the Bijápur viceroy[2]. The most noteworthy point connected with the A'dil Khán dynasty is the fact that Shiváji, the founder of the Marátha empire, was its subject, and that his first successful efforts towards the great aim of his life were made in its dominions. This is not the place for a detailed history of the Bijápur kings; but the most important events connected with them will be briefly noted, special prominence being given to such as relate to the Southern Marátha Country.

Contact with the Portugues and French, A.D. 1510 and A.D. 1674.

In A.D. 1510 Yúsuf A'dil Khán died, leaving a son, Ismail, who at the time of his father's death was too young to assume the reins of government. Kámál Khán Dakhani was appointed protector, but soon aspired to supplant his master. His arrangements for deposing Ismail A'dil Khán and proclaiming himself king were completed, when he was assassinated by an emissary from the queen-mother.[3] Though Kamál Khán's mother and his son Safdar Jang concealed the fact of his death and attempted to carry out the plot as had been planned, their efforts resulted in the death of Safdar Jang and the complete dispersion of their party.

Yúsuf Succeeded by Ismail, A.D. 1510.

Among those most prominent in the defence of their master was Khúsráo Túrk, who was rewarded with the title of Asad Khán, by which he was always afterwards known, and who received Belgaum as a jáhgir, a town which he did much to strengthen and beautify.[4]

Asad Khán of Belgaum.

No sooner had the young king triumphed over his internal foes than he had to meet a formidable confederacy of the kings of Ahmadnagar Golkonda and Berar, who brought with them the unfortunate Bahamani king, once their sovereign, and his son A'hmad. The confederates were signally defeated near Bijápur, and Máhmúd Sháh, together with his son, fell into the hands of the victor. They were treated with the greatest courtesy, and by the Bahamani king's desire the marriage of Ismail A'dil Khán's sister to prince A'hmad, to whom, as noted above, she had been betrothed was celebrated with great magnificence.

Defeat of Ahmadnagar and Berar.

---

[1] Mountstuart Elphinstone in his History of India (4th Edition page 667) seems to have imagined these to be the permanent limits of the kingdom. The wonder he expressed (page 514 note) that so small a state could have maintained so large a capital would have been diminished had he known the size to which the kingdom attained when at its zenith.

[2] Strictly speaking the land was not granted to the French but purchased by them from Shir Khán Lodi, the governor of the Bijápur king's possessions in those parts. See Malleson's French in India, 20 and 26. Shiváji, when subsequently in the neighbourhood, acknowledged the validity of the transaction and, for a consideration, refrained from harrying Pondicherry. Malleson, 25; Wilks' History of Mysor (Indian Reprint), 25.

[3] This lady, Bubuji Khánam, was the sister of Mukund Ráo, a Marátha chief who had opposed Yúsuf A'dil Khán and was defeated.

[4] Stokes' Account of Belgaum, 24-26; Briggs' Farishtha, III. 45.

HISTORICAL SKETCH, A.D. 1300-1818.

Bijápur Defeated by Vijayanagar, A.D. 1523.

The Bijápur king's next campaign was less successful. He marched to recover Mudgal and Raichur from the Vijayanagar rája. When encamped on the banks of the Krishna, under the influence of intoxication, he made an attempt to cross the river without due precautions in the face of the hostile force. The result was a defeat with great loss, the king himself narrowly escaping, and the army having to return to Bijápur. The Musalmán commander-in-chief having fallen in this expedition his place was conferred on Asad Khán, who received the title of Sipáh Sálár and had many districts added to his estates. The new commander soon proved himself worthy of the honours conferred on him, for in A.D. 1524 he defeated, near Sholápur, the confederate kings of Ahmadnagar and Berar and the regent of Bidar. The confederates were subsequently defeated in detail; and the campaign against Amir Baríd, the regent of Bidar, resulted in the capture of the latter by Asad Khán, who, with consummate daring and address, penetrated the hostile camp at night and carried away Amir Baríd on the bed on which he was lying intoxicated. The result was the capture of Bidar, and the regent became practically the vassal of the Bijápur king. Afterwards he, together with the king of Berar, joined the Bijápur army in an expedition against Vijayanagar, in which the forts of Mudgal and Raichur fell again into the hands of the Musalmáns.

Takes Bidar, A.D. 1524.

Mallu Succeeds Ismáil, A.D. 1534.

Not long after this (A.D. 1534) Ismail Ádil Sháh died, leaving Asad Khán guardian to his son and successor, Mallu. The conduct of this young king soon disgusted his guardian, who retired to Belgaum, and alienated all his friends, his own grandmother Bubuji Khánam even taking part against him. After an inglorious reign of six months he was deposed and blinded, and his brother Ibráhim placed on the throne in his stead. The new king inaugurated his reign by adjuring the Shia tenets of his father and grandfather. Still more important was the radical alteration he effected in the government and in the army by getting rid of foreigners and employing only Dakhanis, this change being further marked by the substitution of Maráthi the language of the country for Persian in the state accounts.

Is Deposed and Succeeded by Ibráhim I.

Helps Vijayanagar.

The first expedition of importance undertaken by Ibráhim Ádil Sháh was to Vijáyanagar, where various intrigues and revolutions had been going on which ended in Bhoj Tirmal Rai seizing the throne. The usurper finding his position precarious invited the aid of the Bijápur king, to whom he offered allegiance and large sums of money. The offer was accepted, and Ibráhim in person seated the Hindu prince on the throne of Vijayanagar as his feudatory. This aid proved of little use to Bhoj Tirmal Rai, who, after the departure of his new allies, was attacked by his rebellious subjects and committed suicide to avoid falling into their hands. Shortly after this Asad Khán was sent to attack the fort of Adoni, but concluded peace with Vijayanagar without taking it.[1] Asad Khán in addition to his other offices was now made prime minister. When in the very height of favour he nearly fell, owing to an intrigue, but afterwards the confidence of the king was restored. It was fortunate for Ibráhim that this was the case, as

[1] Briggs' Farishtah, III. 80-86.

a formidable confederacy against him was formed by the kings of Ahmadnagar and Golkonda, and Rám Ráj, the new king of Vijayanagar, who simultaneously attacked him on the north, east, and south. In these critical circumstances the king sent for Asad Khán, who managed to buy off for a time the kings of Ahmadnagar and Vijayanagar, and then marched against and defeated the Golkonda prince, who was thus isolated from his allies. Shortly after war again broke out with Ahmadnagar, and the Bijápur troops under Asad Khán were once more victorious.[1]

HISTORICAL SKETCH, A.D. 1300-1818.

Defeats Golkonda, A.D. 1536.

Élated by victory Ibráhim behaved in such a way as to alienate his friends and leave openings for his enemies to attack him. The Ahmadnagar king took advantage of the prevalent disaffection to renew hostilities; and as Ibráhim only went on to further acts of frantic folly a conspiracy was set on foot to depose him and place his brother Abdulla on the throne. The plot was discovered and Abdulla had to fly to Goa. The king's suspicions were then directed against Asad Khán, who had to betake himself to Belgaum. Notwithstanding the treatment he had received at the hands of his king Asad Khán rejected the offers made to him by Abdulla, who was advancing, supported by the Portuguese from Goa and by Burhán Nizám of Ahmadnagar, who had halted at Miraj on his way to Bijápur. Feeling death approaching the faithful minister invited Ibráhim to visit Belgaum. The invitation was accepted, but before the king's arrival Asad Khán expired (A.D. 1540), having the satisfaction of knowing on his deathbed, that his loyalty and advice had saved his sovereign, for Abdulla's rebellion collapsed and the Ahmadnagar king had to retreat.[2] The rebel prince again took refuge with the Portuguese and thereby brought on hostilities between them and Bijápur, but was killed in A.D. 1554. Ibráhim Ádil Khán did not long enjoy peace. An alliance was made between Burhán Nizám Sháh of Ahmadnagar and the rája of Vijayanagar and hostilities broke out against the Bijápur king and his ally, Áli Baríd of Bidar. Kalyán, belonging to the latter, was besieged by the Ahmadnagar troops, and Ibráhim marched to relieve it. At first he met with some success, but he was taken by surprise by a sudden attack on his camp and had to fly for his life, narrowly escaping capture. In the following year he lost Sholápur, Mudgal, and Raichur, the two last places falling into the hands of their old possessors, the rájás of Vijayanagar.

Abdulla's Rebellion.

Asad Khán Dies, A.D. 1540.

Bijápur Reverses.

Shortly after this the belligerent sovereigns changed parts. On the death of Burhán Nizám Sháh, his successor Hussain made peace with Ibráhim, but the latter, in the hope of recovering Sholápur, espoused the cause of Hussain Sháh's brother and rival, Áli, and further concluded a treaty with Vijayanagar. The Bijápur king trusted much to the aid to be derived from Seif-ain-ul-Mulk, the commander-in-chief of the late king of Ahmadnagar, who had entered his service. A battle

---

[1] Briggs' Farishtah, III. 93-94.

[2] Briggs' Farishtah, 100-101. Mr. Stokes in his Account of Belgaum gives all the details narrated by Farishtah and also (page 34) some traditions about Asad Khán.

HISTORICAL SKETCH, A.D. 1300-1818.

Defeat by Sholápur, A.D. 1556.

ensued near Sholápur, which would have been won by Bijápur had Seif-ain-ul-Mulk been properly supported by Ibráhim Ádil Sháh. The latter fancying himself betrayed, fled from the field; and when the gallant commander-in-chief, after cutting his way through the enemy, arrived at Bijápur, he met with such a reception from the king that he retired to his estates, where he made himself master of the tract watered by the river Mán, and of Válva, Miraj, and other districts. So powerful did Seif-ain-ul-Mulk become, that after he had defeated a royal force sent against him, the king marched against him in person to meet with the same fate, and to be pursued to his capital.

Saved by Vijayanagar.

Nothing would now have saved Bijápur from capture had not the brother of the rája of Vijayanagar, to whom Ibráhim had applied for aid, opportunely arrived and put the besiegers to flight.[1] Not long after this (A.D. 1557) Ibráhim Ádil Sháh died.

Ibráhim Dies, A.D. 1557.

At the time of Ibráhim's death, as they had incurred their father's displeasure by their devotion to the Shia tenets, his two sons were in confinement; the elder, Áli, in the fort of Miraj, and the second, Támásp, in Belgaum. When Ibráhim's life was despaired of Muhammad Kishwar Khán, son of Asad Khán and governor of the districts of Hukkeri, Ráybág, and Belgaum, a man of great influence, moved towards Miraj to secure the succession to prince Áli.

Succeeded by Ali I.

This step enabled the latter, on his father's death, to mount the throne without opposition; and he rewarded the services of Kishwar Khán by making him commander-in-chief. His first object was to get Sholápur out of the hands of the Ahmadnagar king, and he sent an embassy to endeavour to effect this purpose, Kishwar Khán being sent at the same time to Vijayanagar to negotiate a treaty of alliance with Rám Ráj. The latter embassy was more successful than the other; and so close became the alliance between Bijápur and Vijáyanagar, that Áli Ádil Khán paid a visit to Rám Ráj, whose wife adopted him as her son. In the following year the two kings invaded Ahmadnagar, where they met with complete success. Hussain Nizám Sháh managed after a time to buy off the Bijápur king, but immediately afterwards, relying on the aid of the Golkonda king, renewed hostilities. The result was that he was again attacked by the Bijápur and Vijayanagar forces,

Bijápur and Vijayanagar Allied.

which were joined by the Golkonda king who threw over his ally, and the town of Ahmadnagar was besieged by the three kings. Owing to various causes, one of the principal being the disgust of the Musalmáns at the conduct of the Hindu prince and his forces, the siege was raised and Rám Ráj returned to his own dominions, which he had considerably augmented at the cost of his allies.[2]

Musalmán Confederation against Vijayanagar, A.D. 1564.

The insolent conduct of the Vijáyanagar king on this occasion and the outrages which his followers had offered to all that the Musalmáns held most sacred, led to his fall, just when his kingdom seemed to have attained the highest pitch of aggrandisement. His late allies, whom he had insulted and despoiled, formed an alliance with their recent enemy the Ahmadnagar king, which was joined by Ali Barid Sháh of

---

[1] Farishtah, III. 105-111. [2] Farishtah, III. 123.

HISTORICAL SKETCH, A.D. 1300-1818.

Battle of Tálikot: Overthrow of Vijayanagar, A.D. 1565.

Bidar. The bonds between Bijápur and Ahmadnagar were drawn close by the marriage of Áli Ádil Sháh to Chánd Bibi, daughter of Hussain Nizám Sháh, who brought the fort of Sholápur as her dowry; and the four Musalmán sovereigns agreed to combine their forces and attack Rám Ráj, the common enemy of themselves and their religion. The result of the expedition was the complete defeat, at the battle of Tálikot (A.D. 1565) of Rám Ráj, who lost his life, and the eventual subversion of the Vijayanagar kingdom. The territory did not at once fall completely into the hands of the Musalmáns, as Rám Ráj's brother was allowed to retain much territory, and for a considerable time many feudatory chiefs were able to maintain their independence in their provinces. Some districts, such as Terdál, Yádvád, and Torgal, now forming part of the Southern Marátha Country, seem to have been added about this time to the territories of Bijápur.

Áli meets with Defeats.

On the death not long afterwards of Hussain Nizám Sháh, who left a successor still in his minority, Áli Ádil Sháh, in the hope of gaining a further slice of Vijayanagar, interfered in the intestine disputes of that state and espoused the cause of Tim Ráj, the son of Rám Ráj, against Venkatadri, the latter's brother.[1] Venkatadri, however, by an adroit appeal to the jealousy of Ahmadnagar, procured an invasion of Bijápur territory from that quarter, which made Áli Ádil Sháh return with precipitation. Hostilities then ensued between Bijápur and Ahmadnagar in the course of which Kishwar Khán was killed and the Bijápur troops met with great reverses. The same bad fortune attended an expedition to recover Goa from the Portuguese; but Áli Ádil Sháh retrieved his military reputation by taking the famous fort of Adoni, which had been considered impregnable.

But Takes Adoni.

Invades the Southern Marátha Country, A.D. 1573.

The Bijápur king proceeded at once to make good use of the strong position thus obtained in the south. Having secured himself by an agreement with Mortaza Nizám Sháh against intervention on the side of Ahmadnagar, he set to work (A.D. 1573) to recover the conquests that had been made by Firoz Sháh Bahamani some sixty-seven years before. The first place taken was Torgal,[2] which was in the hands of Venkati Yesav Rai, an officer of the Bijápur government who had revolted. Thence the king moved to Dhárwár, which was held by an officer of the late Rám Ráj who had assumed practical independence. Dhárwár fell after a siege of six months; and then the Bijápur troops moved against Bankápur, then the capital of Velápa Rai, who had formerly been a servant of the Vijayanagar king but was now independent. After vain applications for aid to Venkatadri, the brother of his former master, Velápa Rai defended himself with such vigour that he nearly forced his enemy to raise the siege. The Musalmáns were especially annoyed by night attacks, which are thus described by

Takes Dhárwár.

---

[1] Penkonda was now the capital of what remained of the kingdom, Vijáyanagar having been destroyed after the battle of Tálikot. Briggs' Farishtah, III. 131; Wilks' Mysor, 12-31.

[2] Farishtah (Briggs, III. 135) writes the name Toorkul, but it is more than probable that the place named in the text is indicated. Torgal is to the south of Kaládgi, a little off the road from Bijápur to Dhárwár.

HISTORICAL SKETCH, A.D. 1300-1818.

Áli takes Bankápur, A.D. 1575.

Farishtah: "The infantry of the Karnátak, who value their lives but little, were quite naked, and had their bodies anointed with oil to prevent their being easily seized: thus prepared they entered the tents at night and stabbed the soldiers while sleeping without mercy." These attacks occasioned a panic, which would have led to disastrous results, especially as the supplies of the besieging force were also cut off by the activity of the enemy. Mustápha Khán, the Bijápur general, however, by a judicious use of his Bárgirs or Marátha cavalry, re-opened his lines of communication, and by a strong cordon of sentries round the camp effectually checked the night attacks. The result was that after a siege of one year and three months Bankápur was surrendered; and thus nine or ten years after the battle of Tálikot, the whole of the Southern Marátha Country was absorbed into Bijápur.

Conquest South of the Tungbhadra.

Áli Ádil Sháh remained for some time at Bankápur, and from there made successive attacks on the Hindus of the south, in which Mustápha Khán, who was made the head of all departments of the state, greatly distinguished himself. The Hindu chiefs of Malabár and Kánara seem to have submitted generally and to have become tributaries.[1] The Musalmáns were much assisted in these campaigns by their Marátha allies or feudatories, but events proved that the latter were not always to be relied on. After overrunning much country south of the Tungbhadra the Bijápur king turned his arms against Venkatadri, whose capital was blockaded. The city was on the point of falling when Venkatadri managed to gain over Hundiatum Náik, the chief of the Bárgirs, whom he induced by large bribes to desert the king and harass his camp. This was done so effectually that Áli Ádil Sháh had to raise the siege and retire to his own dominions. The conduct of the Maráthás on this occasion was not forgotten or forgiven. Shortly after the Bárgirs committed excesses in their jáhgirs about Vijáyanagar, and a force had to be sent against them, which they resisted successfully for a year. Artifice at last effected what force had failed to accomplish. The insurgents were invited to court, and notwithstanding the warnings of the more prudent among them the greater number accepted the invitation. The result is concisely told by Farishtah: For some time the king treated the Bárgirs with kindness, but at length put most of them to death.[2]

According to the Portuguese historian, epitomised in Briggs' Farishtah,[3] the kings of Ahmadnagar and Bijápur were not very successful in an attack which they made on Goa in conjunction with the ruler of Kálikat in A.D. 1570. Áli Ádil Sháh, it is stated, descended the Phonda pass with a large army and invested Goa, but after ten months was obliged to raise the siege, having lost twelve thousand men besides numbers of elephants and horses. Not long after this a Bijápur vessel having been taken by the Portuguese, the ambassador from that nation to Bijápur was confined in Belgaum till reparation was made.

1 Briggs' Farishtah, III. 138-140. See also Wilks' Mysor, 39.
2 Briggs' Farishtah, III. 141.
3 Farishtah, III. 520.

HISTORICAL SKETCH, A.D. 1300-1818.

In A.D. 1580 A'li met with his death under circumstances most disgraceful to himself, and was succeeded by his nephew Ibráhim. During A'li's reign he did much for the adornment of the capital, the Juma Masjid, the Hauz-i-Shápur, the city wall, and various aqueducts having been constructed by his orders.[1]

Ibráhim II. A.D. 1580. Plots and Counterplots.

Ibráhim A'dil Sháh II. being but nine years of age when his uncle died, the management of the state devolved on Kámil Khán Dakhani and the famous Chánd Bibi, the widow of the late king. As usual under such circumstances a series of palace intrigues and revolutions ensued. Kámil Khán made himself obnoxious and was deposed and killed by Háji Kishwar Khán, who succeeded to his place. The change however was found to be one from King Log to King Stork. The new regent aimed at sole and uncontrolled authority and shrank from no steps to attain his object. Learning that there was some talk of getting Mustápha Khán from Bankápur to oppose him he had the latter assassinated. He next proceeded to rid himself of Chánd Bibi, which he did by getting her confined in the fort of Sátára on the pretence that she had instigated her brother the king of Ahmadnagar to invade Bijápur. His power was but short-lived. A confederacy of the Abyssinian officers of the army was formed and Kishwar Khán had to fly. Chánd Bibi was released, and Yeklás Khán, the head of the Abyssinian party, was associated with her in the regency.

Bijápur Besieged.

The successful party was too unpopular to maintain their position. A formidable confederacy was formed against Bijápur by Ahmadnagar Golkonda and Berar, and the capital was besieged by their forces. Two influential nobles of the Bijápur court joined the besiegers, and the Abyssinians finding their tenure of power insecure consented to an addition to the ministry. Chánd Bibi accordingly called to her council Sháh Abul Hassan, who set to work with marvellous energy and success to free the state from its difficulties. The Marátha chiefs of the Karnátak who had revolted were recalled to their allegiance and summoned to Bijápur, where they did good service by hanging on the rear of the besiegers and cutting off their supplies. The Musalmán leaders who had deserted returned; and so successful were the efforts of the new minister that ere long the invaders found their position untenable. After having sat for twelve months before Bijápur and made a large breach the confederate armies had to raise the siege.

Siege Raised.

The Nizám Sháh army returned to Ahmadnagar, plundering on the way the districts of Kolhár, Hukkeri, Ráybág, Miraj, and Panhála,[2] while some of the Golkonda troops remained in Bijápur territory. The latter were defeated by a Bijápur force under Diláwar Khán, who pursued them to the very gates of their capital.

Diláwar Khán Dictator.

The successful general returned to Bijápur to grasp at supreme power. He seized and blinded Yeklás Khán and Sháh Abul Hassan,

[1] Briggs' Farishtah, III. 143. [2] Briggs' Farishtah, III. 154 and 443.

Diláwar Khán in Power, A.D. 1583-1591.

the latter of whom was afterwards put to death; and all obstacles having been removed and the Abyssinians banished, Diláwar Khán became regent, a position which he held for eight years.

Bad as were the means by which Diláwar Khán attained this position he unquestionably made good use of his power, and his strong hand was soon felt in all parts. The dissensions at the capital had encouraged the recently subdued tributaries in the Karnátak to resume their independence, and operations against them were now begun without delay. A treaty was concluded with Ahmadnagar, which was cemented by the marriage of Ibráhim A'dil Sháh's sister to Hussain, the son of Murtaza Nizám Sháh,[1] and the young Bijápur king was afterwards married to the sister of the Golkonda sovereign.

His Yoke Thrown Off.

The thraldom in which Ibráhim A'dil Sháh was kept by the imperious minister soon became intolerable, and Diláwar Khán's conduct to the king during a subsequent campaign against Ahmadnagar made the latter resolve to gain his independence. Accordingly he suddenly left the minister's camp one morning and repaired to that of certain malcontent nobles; and Diláwar Khán, after a vain attempt to get the king again into his power, had to fly to Ahmadnagar. Peace was made with the latter state for a time, but war soon broke out again owing to the instigation of Diláwar Khán; and Burhán Nizám Sháh invaded Bijápur territory and repaired a ruined fort on the Bhíma where he established himself. Ibráhim A'dil Sháh at first temporised and treated with Diláwar Khán till he got him into his power, when he blinded him and sent him for life to the fort of Sátára.

Invasion from Ahmadnagar Repelled, A.D. 1592.

The king then marched against the invader, whose supplies he cut off by a judicious use of his Marátha cavalry. Finally, harassed by attacks from without and conspiracies from within, Burhán Nizám Sháh was obliged to sue for peace and had to undergo the humiliation of himself dismantling the fort he had re-built in Bijápur territory (A.D. 1592.)

Rebellion of the King's Brother.

Ibráhim A'dil Sháh next turned his arms to the south and made a most successful campaign into the Karnátak and Malabár,[2] when he was recalled by a revolt raised by his brother Ismail, who had been confined as a state-prisoner in the fort of Belgaum. The king at first offered a pardon to the rebel, but as his offers were rejected he sent a force to attack him. Disaffection had spread widely. Some of the leading nobles turned traitors, and the garrison of Miraj revolted and declared for Ismail. To add to the difficulty of the situation, at the instigation of the rebels Burhán Nizám Sháh of Ahmadnagar invaded Bijápur from the north, while the Hindus of Malabár attacked the districts about Bankápur on the south. The army sent against Belgaum returned to Bijápur without orders, and Ain-ul-Mulk, the chief partizan of prince Ismail, joined the latter with an army of thirty thousand men and advanced towards the capital. Hámid Khán, who was sent against the insurgents, pre-

---

[1] Chánd Bibi accompanied her niece to Ahmadnagar, where she afterwards immortalised herself by her heroic defence of the place against the Mughals.

[2] The fort of Mysor was taken on this occasion. Briggs' Farishtah, III. 17.

HISTORICAL SKETCH, A.D. 1300-1818

tended at first to be ready to join their cause, and having thus put them off their guard attacked and defeated them. Ain-ul-Mulk was killed in the action, and Ismail was taken and shortly after was put to death. Ibráhim Ádil Sháh, freed from internal foes, was able to turn his attention towards his foreign enemies. In a campaign against Ahmadnagar Ibráhim Nizám Sháh, the son and successor of Burhán Nizám Sháh, was defeated and killed, and the expedition against the Hindu invaders of the south having been equally successful, Ibráhim Ádil Sháh entered Bijápur in triumph (A.D. 1596).

Ismail's Rebellion Crushed, A.D. 1596.

Interference with Ahmadnagar.

About this time the king sent a force to Ahmadnagar to aid his aunt Chánd Bibi in her defence of that city against the Mughals under Murád, son of the emperor Akbar, who had been invited by one of the factions that convulsed that unhappy kingdom; but the Bijápur troops did not come into collision with the Mughals, who had raised the siege three days before their arrival. Ibráhim Ádil Sháh then arbitrated on the claims of various pretenders to the throne of Ahmadnagar, and for a time peace was restored to that distracted kingdom. The intervention of the Bijápur king was soon again called for and on this occasion his troops came into collision with the Mughals and were defeated. The victors did not follow up their advantage; but afterwards Ibráhim Ádil Sháh sent an embassy to Akbar, and his daughter was married to prince Dániál, the emperor's son, who had succeeded Murád in command of the army of the Dakhan. A secret partition treaty[1] is said to have been executed between Akbar and the Bijápur king, by which the latter was to gain a considerable slice of Ahmadnagar territory. It was probably in consequence of this that Ibráhim Ádil Sháh resisted with short-sighted policy the consolidation of Ahmadnagar under Malik Amber.[2] The rivalry between the two ended only with their deaths, which took place within a year of each other. Ibráhim Ádil Sháh died in A.D. 1626, leaving to his son and successor Muhammad a full treasury and a powerful army. Every one who has seen Bijápur will remember his exquisite mausoleum, the Ibráhim Roza, which stands on a raised stone platform outside the town faced by a mosque of corresponding style and dimensions.

Ibráhim Dies, A.D. 1626.

Muhammad Ádil Sháh, A.D. 1626.

When Muhammad Ádil Sháh succeeded his father, Sháh Jahán was on the throne of the Mughals, and the Bijápur king at first avoided anything that might bring him into collision with the great northern power. He soon changed his policy. Notwithstanding the terrible famine which was devastating the country, owing to a failure of the periodical rains in A.D. 1629 and the following year, Ázam Khán, Sháh Jahán's general, carried on operations against Ahmadnagar, which was brought to the brink of ruin. The position of the rival state

[1] Grant Duff, I. 77.

[2] At this point we lose the invaluable guidance of the historian Farishtah. The loss, however, is of the less importance that the historical interest at this period is concentrated not so much on the internal history of Bijápur as on the gradual approach of the Mughals and on the rise of the Maráthás, which jointly brought about the destruction of the Ádil Khán dynasty and kingdom.

HISTORICAL SKETCH, A.D. 1500-1818.

Alliance with Ahmadnagar, A.D. 1629.

was at first not unpleasing to Muhammad Ádil Sháh, but afterwards he began to perceive what would be the probable consequence to himself of the subversion of the Nizám Sháh kingdom by the Mughals. He accordingly made an alliance with Murtaza Nizám Sháh, and sent an army under his general, Randullah Khán, which engaged the Mughals and was defeated. At the same time the Ahmadnagar king was assassinated and his state placed at the mercy of the Mughals by the traitor Fatih Khán, so that Sháh Jahán was enabled to direct his whole attention to Bijápur.

Bijápur Invaded by the Mughals.

The territory was invaded by an army under Asaf Khán, but the general found it no easy task to take his capital, as the Bijápur king displayed considerable talents both as a soldier and as a diplomatist. While amusing Asaf Khán with pretended negotiations and feigned offers, he arranged so that his supplies were cut off, and finally the Mughal leader had to raise the siege. He accordingly retired, but in revenge plundered and destroyed the country as far west as Miraj. The Bijápur troops then took the aggressive and attacked the Mughal forces which were besieging Daulatábád, but met with a defeat.

Muhammad Ádil Sháh then made some attempts at negotiation which were not favourably received. Some time after an ambassador was sent from Sháh Jahán[1] calling on the Bijápur king to give up forts belonging to Ahmadnagar which had fallen into his hands, to surrender his guns and military stores, and to cease affording countenance to the famous partizan leader, Sháhji Bhonsle,[2] who had done so much to avert the ruin of the Ahmadnagar kingdom. The rejection of these demands brought on war. Sháhji, driven out of the Ahmadnagar territory, fled into that of Bijápur, in consequence of which the country about Kolhápur, Miraj, and Ráybág was utterly wasted by the Mughals. Another force attacked the capital of Bijápur, but found that in anticipation of its arrival all the forage and grain within a circuit of twenty miles round the fort had been destroyed and the wells filled up. As a regular siege was impracticable, the invading forces marched through the country in two bodies, plundering and devastating. In these operations they met with some loss from attacks by the Bijápur troops; but Muhammad Ádil Sháh was at last compelled to sue for peace. He received more favourable terms than might have been expected, the harshest condition being the imposition of a tribute of twenty lákhs a year. Peace was concluded in A.D. 1636. In the following year, on the complete subversion of the Ahmadnagar kingdom, Sháhji Bhonsle entered the service of Bijápur.

Country Devastated.

Peace with the Mughals, A.D. 1636.

The services of the new adherent were soon utilised. Sháhji having been confirmed in the jáhgir of Poona, which he had received

---

[1] The great gun at Bijápur called the Malak-i-Maidán or Monarch of the Plain was specifically demanded on this occasion. It weighs 40 tons, but is only 15 feet long; the muzzle is 4 feet 8 inches in diameter and the calibre 2 feet 4 inches. It was cast at Ahmadnagar in A.D. 1549, and is supposed to have been taken by Áli Ádil Sháh in A.D. 1562. See Briggs' Farishtah, III. 239 Note and 243 Note: also Grant Duff's Maráthás, I. 83 Note.

[2] The father of the great Shiváji.

from his late masters, was sent, under Randullah Khán, on an expedition into what is now the Madras Presidency, where he was promised a large jáhgir, which he afterwards received. He was completely successful and extended the limits of the Bijápur kingdom to the Bay of Bengal.[1]

Sháhji Arrested as a Traitor.

While Sháhji was thus engaged, his son Shiváji, who had been left at Poona, laid the foundations of his future power by getting into his possession several forts belonging to Bijápur. His proceedings at first were little noticed, but when fort after fort fell into his hands the rebellion was too serious to be overlooked. Persuaded that Shiváji was carrying out instructions received from Sháhji, the king sent orders to Báji Ghorpadĕ, jáhgirdár of Mudhol, who was serving with the latter in the Karnátak, to seize the rebel's father. This was effected by treachery, and Sháhji was sent a prisoner to Bijápur. Here he was desired to suppress his son's rebellion; and his assurances that Shiváji had been acting in contravention of his wishes and that he was unable to restrain him were disbelieved. He was accordingly shut in a stone dungeon the door of which was built up, leaving only a small opening, and he was assured that this also would be closed if his son did not submit.

But Finally Released.

On hearing of his father's precarious situation Shiváji applied for aid to the emperor Sháh Jahán, who agreed to admit him into the imperial service and brought such influence to bear on Bija'pur that Sháhji was released from his dungeon. He was however kept a prisoner at large for four years until the growing disturbances in the Karnátak rendered it necessary to send him there. Before dismissing him Muhammad A'dil Sháh bound him over to refrain from molesting the Mudholkar, and a nominal reconciliation was brought about. Sháhji however, so far from being reconciled, charged his son by his filial duty to punish Báji Ghorpadé, an injunction not neglected by Shiváji, who some years afterwards made a sudden descent on Mudhol, which he burnt, killing at the same time his father's enemy.

Mu'ammed Dies. Succeeded by A'li II. A.D. 1656.

Ever since the peace of A.D. 1636, Muhammad A'dil Sháh had kept on good terms with the Mughal emperor. Unfortunately for his successor he cultivated the favour of Sháh Jahan's eldest son Dára Shekoh, a fact which spurred on to fiercer zeal Aurangzíb, who had, on other grounds, resolved to reduce Bijápur to the condition of a province of the empire. The storm however did not burst during the life-time of Muhammad A'dil Sháh, who died quietly at his capital in A.D. 1656. His tomb, surmounted by one of the largest domes in the world, is the most prominent object seen when approaching or leaving Bijápur.

Bija'pur Besieged

A'li A'dil Sháh II., son of the late king, succeeded to a troubled heritage at the age of nineteen. His claim to the throne was disputed by the Mughals without any valid grounds; and an army under

---

1 In 1638 Randullah Kha'n besieged Saringapatan, but was repulsed. He subsequently took Bangalor, which Sháhji afterwards made his head-quarters. For the Bijápur conquests in the south of this period see Wilks' Mysor, I. 41, 42, and 49. About this time Tánjor was taken either by Sháhji or his son Venka'ji.

Historical Sketch, A.D. 1300-1818.

Bijápur Saved for the time, A.D. 1657.

Aurangzíb marched against his capital. Khán Muhammad the prime minister, who was sent against the invaders, allowed himself to be bought over, and aided instead of resisting the approach of the Mughals. The siege was at once formed and carried on with vigour, and nothing could have saved the city, when Aurangzíb heard of the supposed mortal illness of his father Sháh Jahán. Feeling it necessary for the prosecution of his designs to be present at the death-bed, he hastily made peace with the young king, and evacuated the Bijápur territory.

Campaign against Shiváji.

Left to itself the city became a prey to factions, and the position of the youthful prince, surrounded by intriguing adherents, many of whom were also traitors, was most difficult.[1] Khán Muhammad was assassinated, and an army was sent under Afzúl Khán against Shiváji, who, after treacherously killing the leader, destroyed the force in the jungles under Mahábaleshvar. A more detailed account of the proceedings of Shiváji at this period will be found in the historical account of the state of Kolhápur. Suffice it to say here, that aided probably by the treachery of Rustum Zamán, an officer of the Bijápur government in charge of the Miraj and Panhála districts, the Marátha leader was enabled to plunder to the gates of Bijápur; and when the approach of the Bijápur troops forced him to take refuge in the fort of Panhála, he escaped. The king then took the field in person, and after capturing Panhála and Pávangad proceeded south to restore order in the Karnátak. On the way he had to take the forts of Raichur and Torgal, and when encamped on the Tungbhadra he was attacked by the rebel Sidi Johár, formerly an officer in his service. He remained two years in the Karnátak with his army, leaving the northern part of his kingdom at the mercy of Shiváji, who did not fail to take advantage of the opportunity thus afforded. Such was the condition of the once proud Bijápur monarchy that Áli Ádil Sháh was obliged to consent to a peace which left Shiváji in possession of the Konkan from Kalyán to Goa, and of a strip of country above the Sahyádris extending from the north of Poona to the south of Miraj (A.D. 1662).

Campaign in the Karnátak.

Humiliating Peace with Shiváji, A.D. 1662.

Renewed Hostilities, A.D. 1664.

The peace thus purchased was of short duration. Two years later the Bijápur generals at Panhála made an attempt to recover the Konkan and were defeated by Shiváji, who further revenged himself by sending his horse to plunder the Bijápur territory. He afterwards entered into an offensive alliance with the Mughals against Áli Ádil Sháh, and joined the army of Jaisingh, Aurangzíb's general, in an invasion of the Bijápur dominions. Shiváji after a time left Jaisingh to pay a visit to Delhi, while the Mughals, who advanced to Bijápur, were so harassed by the Dakhan horse and suffered so much from sickness and from want of water and supplies that they had to raise the siege. Not long after Áli Ádil Sháh concluded a treaty with Aurangzíb to the advantage of the latter; and the pretensions and

Bijápur again Besieged.

Peace with the Mughals.

---

[1] A graphic account of the condition of Bijápur at this time will be found in the late Colonel Meadows Taylor's Tara. Though avowedly a work of fiction the historical details in the book are correct and the local colouring perfect.

Ali Dies. Succeeded by Sikandar a Minor, A.D. 1672.

attacks of Shiváji were bought off by agreeing to pay him three lákhs of rupees annually. At the end of A.D. 1672 the Bijápur king died, leaving a son, Sultán Sikandar, then only in his fifth year. On his death-bed A'li A'dil Sháh appointed as regent Kháwas Khán, son of the traitorous prime minister whose assassination has been noted above, and suggested that the leading nobles should be put in charge of the several districts, the Southern Marátha Country being assigned to Abdul Karim the ancestor of the Sávanur nawábs. The regent, however, though he assented to these arrangements, refrained from giving them effect for fear of his subordinates making their own terms with the Mughals when at a distance from the capital.

Marátha Attacks.

Shiváji was not likely to neglect the opportunity offered to him by the infancy of the king and the factions at Bijápur. He at once declared war, retook Panhála, and sent an expedition which sacked the rich town of Húbli, on its way plundering Belgaum.[1] These and other attacks led to an army being sent against the Maráthás under Abdul Karim, who regained possession of the open country about Panhála. While he was thus employed a Marátha force appeared in the neighbourhood of Bijápur and plundered with impunity. Abdul Karim was recalled to the defence of the capital, and between Miraj and Bijápur was attacked by the Maráthás and obliged to come to terms. Shortly afterwards, thinking he saw an opportunity of retaking Panhála, he again advanced with an army in that direction. He defeated the Maráthás under Pratáp Ráo near Panhála, but while his troops were dispersed in pursuit he was attacked by a fresh body and routed, after which he retired in disgrace to Bijápur.

Shiváji Enthroned, A.D. 1674.

In this year (A.D.1674), Shiváji, who had long previously assumed royal titles and struck coins in his name, was formally enthroned with great ceremony.

Mughal Attack.

In the following year the regent Kháwas Khán opened negotiations with the Mughals and agreed to hold Bijápur as a dependent province of the empire. He also arranged to give the young king's sister in marriage to one of the sons of Aurangzíb. The proposed measures however were most unpalatable to the nobles and people of Bijápur, and when the regent's negotiations became known a conspiracy was formed against him and he was assassinated. The chief authority then fell into the hands of Abdul Karim, who acted with such vigour, that when the Mughals appeared to receive the surrender of Bijápur they were attacked and worsted in several actions; and finally a treaty was made on terms honourable to Bijápur.[2]

---

[1] Grant Duff's Maráthás, I. 188; Stokes' Belgaum, 42. This is the first occasion on which we hear of Shiváji or his troops operating much to the south of Kolhapur; yet according to tradition he had twelve years previously built, among others, the forts of Rámdurg and Nargund. See A Memoir of the State of the Southern Marátha Country by Captain E. W. West. Selection from Bombay Government Records, CXIII, New Series, 173. Had, however, these forts been in existence and in Marátha hands at the time of A'li A'dil Sháh's expedition to the Karnátak, just noted, we should have heard of their being besieged by him.

[2] Grant Duff's Maráthás, I. 195.

HISTORICAL SKETCH, A.D. 1300-1818.

Shiváji in the Karnátak, A.D. 1676.

In the next year (A.D. 1676) Shiváji made his famous expedition into the Karnátak. He first went to Golkonda, where he concluded a treaty hostile to Bijápur and the new regent. He then proceeded to the south, where he recovered the jáhgir that had been granted to his father and plundered or took the other districts belonging to Bijápur in that quarter. In the meantime Abdul Karim, with the Mughals, proceeded to attack Golkonda in revenge for the treaty made with Shiváji. The expedition was unsuccessful, and to add to the difficulties of the situation Abdul Karim died. He was succeeded by Musáud Khán, an Abyssinian, who owed his appointment to Dilír Khán the Mughal general, and who consequently favoured the Mughal faction. The new regent did not display much generalship or statesmanlike ability. He dismissed a large portion of the cavalry who took service with the enemies of Bijápur, and before long he had the mortification of seeing the whole Southern Marátha Country overrun by Shiváji's troops. He was further pressed by the Mughals under Sultán Múazzim, Aurangzíb's son, who demanded Pádsháh Bibi the king's sister. The demand was refused, but as one of the factions in the city was prepared to support it by force, the princess of herself went to the Mughal camp in the hope of saving her brother and country. The sacrifice was of no avail. The siege of Bijápur was pressed, and in his despair the regent applied to Shiváji for aid. The latter at once made a diversion by a vigorous attack on the Mughal possessions in the Dakhan. On a further application from Musáud Khán the Maráthás hovered around the besieging army and cut off its supplies, so that Dilír Khán had to raise the siege. He accordingly marched to the west, plundered Athni, and was laying waste the country to the south of the Krishna when he was again attacked by the Maráthás and forced to retreat. Shiváji, in return for the assistance rendered to Bijápur on this occasion, received a grant of most of the Bijápur possessions in what is now the Madras Presidency. He died shortly afterwards (A.D. 1680) and was succeeded by his son Sambháji.

Bijápur again Besieged.

Siege Raised by Shiváji.

Final Siege by Aurangzíb.

The death of Shiváji and the succession of a prince of a very different type removed a formidable obstacle from the path of Aurangzíb, who was now left free to pursue his designs against Bijápur. His envoy there intrigued and gained over many of the principal officers, and owing to his influence Musáud Khán had to retire. The new administration attempted to recover some of the rich districts on the Krishna that had fallen into Shiváji's possession, and Miraj was re-taken, which occasioned an irreparable breach between Bijápur and Sambháji. Aurangzíb in person now came into the Dakhan and sent his son Sultán Múazzim into the Konkan. The latter afterwards ascended the Gháts, and making Válva his head-quarters for the time, subdued the country round, and then marched to the south, successively taking Gokák, Hubli, and Dhárwár. Prince Azím, another son of Aurangzíb's, had meanwhile advanced against Bijápur, but had been compelled to retire; and a force sent against Sultán Múazzim found his troops so weakened by disease and reduced in numbers by the drafts required to garrison the new acquisitions that he too had to retreat. Another attempt was then made by prince Azím, which was near being as unsuccessful as the first. The last days of the Bijápur monarchy had now come. Aurangzíb having crippled Golkonda, turned his whole efforts against Bijápur, whither he proceeded in person, and after a gallant defence the city was taken (A.D. 1686). The young prince fell into the hands of the conqueror and died in captivity.

HISTORICAL SKETCH, A.D. 1300-1818.

Fall of Bijápur, A.D. 1686.

The subversion of the Bijápur kingdom removes the connecting link which rendered it feasible to give a continuous historical account of the tract of country forming the subject of this sketch. The tide of war too, before long, rolled northwards; and until the latter part of the eighteenth century the Southern Marátha Country was the scene of but few events of sufficient historical importance to be recorded.

Aurangzíb Takes Possession.

After the capture of Bijápur Aurangzíb lost no time in securing possession of the territories that had thus become a portion of his empire. His armies marched to the furthest southern districts belonging to the extinct kingdom—those situated in what was termed the Bijápur Karnátak—driving the Maráthás everywhere into their forts. The Mughal tenure of the country, however, was purely military and did not last long. Abdul Ráuf Khán, son of the deceased Abdul Karim, who has often been referred to in these pages, entered the service of the emperor and received charge of a large portion of the Southern Marátha Country. He first made Bankápur his head-quarters, but eventually carved out for himself a principality the capital of which was Sávanur. Aurangzíb's hands were too fully occupied elsewhere to enable him to look closely after his new acquisitions in the south, which soon ceased to belong to him even in name. In the northern part of the Southern Marátha Country his hold at first seemed to be firm. Miraj and Panhála were taken by the Mughals, but the latter place was almost immediately re-taken by the Maráthás. It fell again into Aurangzíb's hands, but the emperor had to move towards the north, leaving behind an enemy whose power increased daily as that of the Mughal waned. The inevitable end was delayed by the dissensions among the Marátha leaders and the absence from the scene of action of their rája, but at Aurangzíb's death his power in the south was very circumscribed. His son Kám Baksh was at Bijápur when his father died, and tried to revive the Mughal empire there, but was soon defeated and killed.

Sháhu, A.D. 1719.

When Sháhu, the grandson of the great Shiváji, was released by the Mughals, he found the Southern Marátha Country partly overrun by the adherents of his cousin the rája of Kolhápur and partly in the hands of the Sávanur nawáb. He promised to clear his country of plunderers and practically to bring it again under the Mughal emperor if the latter would bestow on him the *chauth* and *sar-deshmukhi* of the six subhás of the Dakhan. His application was at first refused, but in A.D. 1719 he obtained from Delhi the grants above noted, and in addition the *svaráj* or personal sovereignty of a number of districts extending from Poona to a considerable distance south of the Tungbhadra river and comprising the greater part of the dominions of the extinct Bijápur kingdom.[1] Various officers were appointed to

[1] Grant Duff's Maráthás, I. 324-5.

HISTORICAL SKETCH, A.D. 1300-1818.

The Nizám, A.D. 1730.

the several provinces, and the tract of country of which this sketch has to deal was placed under Fateh Sing Bhonsle. Some years later (A.D. 1730) in the treaty between the rájás of Sátára and Kolhápur, the territory lying between the rivers Várna and Krishna on the north and the Tungbhadra on the south was assigned to Kolhápur. Miraj Tásgaon and Athni thus remained with Sháhu; but he and the Peshwás exercised sovereignty over a considerable portion of the tract assigned to Kolhápur by the treaty. The Nizám too divided the revenue with the Maráthás in such parts of the Southern Marátha Country as were not included in the *svaráj* or had not been wholly ceded in jáhgir, and long held Bijápur and the adjacent country. In his capacity of viceroy of the Dakhan he interfered to suppress disturbances in the Bijápur Karnátak,[1] and appointed a new subhedár to that district. He is said to have taken the fort of Belgaum into his own hands about this time and to have kept it for ten years, after which it passed into the hands of the Sávanur nawáb as his deputy.[2]

The Sávanur Nawáb, A.D. 1746.

The great power and extensive territory that the Sávanur nawáb acquired during the various changes noted above is shown by the cessions which Nawáb Majid Khán had to make by treaty to the Peshwa some years after. The *chauth* and *sar-deshmukhi* of the country between the Krishna and Tungbhadra had been farmed out to a well-known banker, Bápu Náik Báramatikar, and, as the latter's authority was resisted, an expedition was sent into the Southern Marátha Country in A.D. 1746 under Sadáshiv Chimnáji Bháu the Peshwa's cousin. It is probable that the obstruction had in a great measure been occasioned by the nawáb, who not long before had thrown off his dependence on the Mughals. Majid Khán, however, was not strong enough to resist the Marátha force and had to agree to a treaty by which he yielded up the whole of the country comprised in the tálukás of Bágalkot, Bádámi, Pádshápur, Kittur, Dhárwár, Navalgund, Parasgad, Dambal, part of Ránebennur and Kod, Gokák, Yádvád, Torgal, Haliyál, and others, thirty-six districts in all. He was allowed to retain Mishrikot, Hubli, Bankápur, Hángal, and other districts, to the number of twenty-two, together with the forts of Bankápur, Torgal, and Azamnagar or Belgaum.[3] The ceded districts seem not to have passed at once into the hands of the Maráthás, as Gokák was taken by the Peshwa on his return from his expedition into the southern Karnátak in A.D. 1754; and later on Bágalkot is mentioned as having been similarly taken.

Has to yield Territory to the Peshwa.

On this last occasion Abdul Khán, the Sávanur nawáb, brought on a conflict which resulted in his losing several more districts. Báláji Báji Ráo, in the year that Gokák was taken, sent another expedition into the Karnátak which he himself accompanied part of the way. In the course of the campaign a Musalmán officer

[1] An account of the territory comprised under the name Bijápur Karnátak is given in Wilks' Mysor, I. 136. [2] Stokes' Belgaum, 47.

[3] Memoir of the Chiefs of the Southern Marátha Country, 208. Belgaum is said to have received the name of Azamnagar from prince Azam, Aurangzíb's second son, who lived there for some time after the fall of Bijápur. Stokes' Belgaum, 45. But the name seems older. See Bombay Gazetteer, XXI. 376 note 8.

HISTORICAL SKETCH, A.D. 1300-1818.

Báji Ráo's Campaign against Sávanur, A.D. 1756.

who had formerly been in the service of the famous French leader Bussy and had subsequently entered that of the Peshwa, took offence and again changed masters, this time taking service with Abdul Khán. The latter refused the demand for his surrender made by Báláji Báji Ráo, and consequently the Peshwa assembled an army and marched against Sávanur. As this movement was regarded with suspicion by the Nizám, who claimed the Sávanur chief as his subject, the co-operation of Salábat Jang was asked by the Peshwa, who represented that Abdul Khán was hostile to both parties. Accordingly, a force from Haidarábád, under Bussy, joined the Maráthás who were besieging Sávanur. The power of the European artillery was soon felt and the nawáb was obliged to submit. By the treaty then made (A.D. 1756) he ceded Mishrikot Hubli and Kundgol and other districts, eleven in all, receiving in compensation the Parasgad táluka and some districts in Ránebennur. To meet the pecuniary fine levied the nawáb had to pledge Bankápur; and it is probable that about this time the fort of Belgaum was given to the Peshwa.[1] The latter seems not to have taken the territory thus acquired under his direct management, but to have left it, for the most part, to the *desáis*, who were held responsible for the revenue.

Bijápur ceded to the Peshwa, A.D. 1760.

Not long afterwards the Peshwa made another valuable acquisition. In A.D. 1760 the fort and province of Bijápur were ceded to him by Nizám Ali. He thus became the master of the whole of the Southern Marátha Country except the portions which belonged to Kolhápur. To check the latter state the fort of Miraj and a *saranjám* were bestowed in 1761 on Govind Hari Patvardhan, who had distinguished himself at the siege of Sávanur. Two years later, when the attacks of Haidar Ali of Saringapatan had to be provided against, territory yielding a revenue of upwards of twenty-five lákhs of rupees was granted in *saranjám* to the Patvardhan. The grant comprised not only the territory occupied by the existing Patvardhan states of Sángli, Miraj, Kurundvád, and Jamkhandi, but also several districts now included in the collectorates of Sátára Belgaum and Dhárwár, which during the last half century have passed into the hands of the British Government by cession or lapse.[2] Besides the territory assigned in *saranjám* the Peshwa subsequently granted to the Patvardhan family the districts of Chikodi and Mánoli, which belonged to, or at all events were claimed by the rája of Kolhápur. During the next fifty years these districts seldom or never remained ten years continuously in the hands of one master, but went backwards and forwards between Kolhápur and the Patvardhan and the Nipáni chief till, in the early part of the present century, they passed into the hands of the British Government under the circumstances narrated in the historical sketch of Kolhápur.

Patvardhan Grant, A.D. 1761.

---

[1] Stokes' Belgaum, 51; Memoir of the States of the Southern Marátha Country, 209; Grant Duff's Maráthás, II. 67.

[2] Some districts to the south of the Tungbhadra, such as Baswa Pattan and Harihar, were included. It was noted in the *Táinát Zabita* or grant-deed that Haidar Ali had brought the first-named district under his rule, the *naïve* remark being added, "If he has not got the máháls then they are with the *sarkár*."

HISTORICAL SKETCH, A.D. 1300-1318.

Between A.D. 1763 and the close of the eighteenth century the most prominent events of which the Southern Marátha Country was the scene were repeated raids by the Patvardhans and the Kolhápur rája on one another's territories; an invasion of the country by the Nizám of Haidarábád; the constant attacks by Haidar Áli and his son Tipu of Mysor on the districts south of the Krishna; and the consequent campaigns against those princes. As far as is necessary, the mutual attacks of the Patvardhans and Kolhápur have been noted in the account of Kolhápur. Of the Nizám's invasion it need only be observed that it was made in A.D. 1774 from Adoni by Basálat Jang, who levied contributions as far as Athni and Miraj but was soon obliged to retire. The invasions of the Mysor princes were much more formidable and call for more detailed notice.

Haidar Áli, A.D. 1759.

The rise of the Mysor "Mayor of the Palace," Haidar Áli, who was to play towards the rájás of that country the part which the Peshwa played towards the rája of Sátára, had been watched jealously by the Maráthás.[1] In A.D. 1759 his expulsion of their troops from some districts which had been pledged to Báláji Báji Ráo brought about a conflict between them in which the Maráthás had the worst of it and were obliged to conclude a treaty on terms not very favourable to themselves.[2] In 1761 Haidar got Basálat Khán to invest him with the title of Nawáb of Sira, a district to the south of the Tungbhadra which was in the possession of the Maráthás. The position of Sávanur rendered the alliance or subjection of that state a matter of importance; and as the nawáb Abdul Hakim Khán remained staunch to his engagements with the Maráthás, hostilities ensued. The nawáb was defeated in 1764 and had to submit to the terms imposed on him; and Haidar, having to return to the south, left an army under Fazl Ullah Khán to spread his conquests northward. As no preparations had been made for resistance the general had an easy task. Dhárwár was taken, and as a result of this conquest a large tract of country to the north of Dhárwár was occupied by Haidar's troops.[3] Great preparations were made at Poona to repel this invasion, and an army marched under the Peshwa Mahádev Ráo towards the scene of action. Gopál Ráo Patvardhan was sent on in advance but was defeated by Fazl Ullah Khán. On the Peshwa's approach the latter had to fall back on Haidar's army, which had advanced to his support, leaving a strong garrison in Dhárwár. The two armies came face to face not far from Sávanur, but Mahádev Ráo declined a general action and occupied himself with driving out Haidar's garrisons from the town and villages north of the Varda. An attempt by Haidar to bring on a battle resulted in his discomfiture, and he had to retreat to his entrenched camp at Anavati. The approach of the rains put a stop to further hostilities

Invades the Southern Marátha Country.

Takes Dhárwár.

[1] Haidar himself drew the parallel on an occasion when the Peshwa's envoy tried to pose as the champion of the legitimate sovereign. An account of this curious conversation is given in Wilks' Mysor, I. 304.

[2] Wilks' Mysor, I. 228-29.

[3] As the line of least resistance was naturally followed, the districts taken were mostly in the present collectorate of Bijápur. The strength of the Belgaum fort seems to have saved the districts covered by it. Stokes' Belgaum, 52.

HISTORICAL SKETCH, A.D. 1300-1818.

Haidar Driven Back, A.D. 1766.

for the time. The Peshwa cantoned his troops at a place called Narnedra; and as soon as the season admitted of active operations, took Dhárwár, and thus completed the recovery of all the country north of the Varda. He then made over the command to his uncle Raghunáth Ráo, who pursued Haidar across the Tungbhadra, and finally made a treaty at Bednur, by which Haidar, among other stipulations, agreed to relinquish all claims on Sávanur.

The peace did not last long, as in 1767 the Peshwa invaded Mysor and Haidar was obliged to buy off his attack, having other formidable enemies to deal with. The breach of the new treaty led to another attack on Haidar a few years later. The Maráthás were successful, but as all the operations were carried on to the south of the Tungbhadra they need not be detailed here. The death of the Peshwa Mahádev Ráo in A.D. 1772, followed by that of his brother Náráyan Ráo in the next year, and the question of the disputed succession to the Peshwa's throne, afforded Haidar an opportunity of regaining the territory which he had been forced to disgorge. He recovered the districts south of the Tungbhadra which had fallen into the hands of the Maráthás and entered into intimate relations with Raghunáth Ráo, the uncle of the late Peshwa and the claimant to the throne, whom he acknowledged as the head of the Maráthás and agreed to support. In A.D. 1776 he was invited by his new ally to take possession of the Southern Marátha Country up to the Krishna, and Haidar understood that he was to retain these districts.[1] Accordingly he crossed the Tungbhadra, took Bankápur and Sávanur, and would doubtless have pushed his arms further north had not the rains put a stop to active operations. He then returned to the south leaving a force to protect his acquisitions. Konhér Ráo Patvardhan was sent against this force, but was defeated, and his relation, Pándurang Ráo, the grandfather of the present chief of Sángli, was taken prisoner. The allied forces of the Maráthás and the Nizám then marched against Haidar, the former under Parsharám Bháu, the most distinguished member of the Patvardhan family, moving towards Sávanur. The Nizám's forces were however bought off, and the Maráthás, after having suffered a repulse, retired. This left the field open to Haidar, who soon took Kopál, Dhárwár, Gajendragad, Bádámi, and other places, the fall of which made him master of the country as far as the Krishna.[2] Many strong places such as Nargund and Kittur he left in the hands of their chiefs, on the latter acknowledging his supremacy and agreeing to pay tribute an arrangement which much facilitated his conquest of the country. Circumstances prevented the Maráthás making an attempt to recover the country thus taken, and so Haidar remained for a time in undisturbed possession. Indeed, his right was acknowledged by the Maráthás not long after, when they wished to secure his aid against the English, and he strengthened his hold of the territory by a close alliance with the nawáb of Sávanur, whose eldest son was married to his eldest daughter, Haidar's second son being at the same time married to Abdul Hakim's daughter (A.D. 1779).

Again Invades the Southern Marátha Country, A.D. 1776.

Takes the country as far North as the Krishna.

[1] Wilks' Mysor, I. 397. Grant Duff (Maráthás, I. 239) doubts that this invitation was given.

[2] Wilks' Mysor, I. 419.

HISTORICAL SKETCH, A.D. 1300-1818.

The Treaty of Sálbái, A. D. 1782.

At the time when the treaty of Sálbái was being negotiated between the English and the Maráthás, Nána Phadnávis the Peshwa's minister endeavoured to persuade Haidar to restore the territory north of the Tungbhadra, and unless his demand was complied with, threatened to join the English against Haidar. But Haidar taking advantage of the rivalry between Nána and Mahádji Sindia was able to protract negotiations, till his death on the 20th of December 1782.

The Poona minister did not lose sight of his cherished design. He called on Tipu for arrears of tribute which the latter acknowledged to be due but evaded paying. Nána then endeavoured to get the Nizám to join him in recovering from the Mysor prince the territory which both states had lost by the encroachments of the latter. Nizám A'li, however, set too high a value on his assistance; and though he was promised Bijápur after the recovery from Tipu of the country north of the Tungbhadra, he refused to co-operate unless Bijápur and Ahmadnagar were made over to him at once. Tipu, on hearing what had taken place, showed his contempt for the Nizám by sending an insulting message in which he claimed to be the sovereign of Bijápur.

War beween Tipu and the Maráthás, A. D. 1784.

The disagreement between the Maráthás and the Nizám for the time prevented any attack on Tipu, but the inevitable conflict was not long delayed. It has been noted above how the chief of Nargund became a tributary of Haidar and was allowed to retain his state on those terms. After Haidar's death Tipu demanded an increased tribute, a demand with which Venkat Ráo, the Nargund chief, was unwilling to comply. As he was unable to resist unless supported, he first made overtures to the Bombay Government, and when these failed, to the court of Poona, where he had interest through the Patvardhans. The result of the latter application was that Nána Phadnávis interposed, and while acknowledging Tipu's right to levy tribute from the Nargundkar denied his right to claim more than the amount previously paid. Tipu's reply to this was the despatch of two bodies of troops to enforce his demands and if they were not complied with to besiege Nargund. A Marátha force despatched to the assistance of the Nargund chief found that, owing to want of water, the Mysor force had been obliged to raise the siege, but was still in the neighbourhood. Skirmishing ensued in which the Maráthás had the worst; and Tipu's troops attacked and took the fort of Rámdurg, not far from Nargund, and then resumed the siege of the latter place. On the assurances of Tipu that only the former tribute would be exacted from the Nargund chief the Marátha force withdrew, after which the siege was pressed with redoubled vigour. Terms were promised to the unfortunate chief on the strength of which he capitulated; but no sooner had he evacuated his fort than, in violation of the agreement, he was seized and sent into captivity with his family, and his daughter was taken into Tipu's harem (A.D. 1785). The fort of Kittur was seized at the same time and garrisoned by Mysor troops. Having thus secured his hold of the country, Tipu, to gratify his bigotry and insult the Hindus, forcibly circumcised large numbers of the inhabitants. In the following year the Maráthás and the Nizám formed an offensive alliance against the Mysor prince, and agreed to open operations by

Forced Circumcision of Hindus by Tipu.

Maráthás and Nizám against Tipu.

taking from him the country between the Krishna and Tungbhadra. Accordingly a force was sent against Tipu's general at Kittur, while the main body of the combined army advanced against Bádámi, which they besieged. The town was taken by assault and the garrison of the fort submitted.[1] The force sent to Kittur was less successful. It succeeded in driving the Mysor troops from the adjacent district, but failed in taking the fort. Holkar, who was in charge of the force, suddenly left Kittur and marched to Sávanur, where he was joined by the nawáb, who, though closely related by marriage to Tipu, had been so badly treated that he willingly espoused the cause of the Maráthás. The combined force repulsed an attack made by Tipu's general and were presently joined by Hari Pant, the Marátha commander-in-chief, who had taken the forts of Gajendragad and Bahádur Benda, and now came to Sávanur to find himself opposed by an army under Tipu in person. Hostilities went on languidly for some time with varying success. Hari Pant took the fortified town of Sirhatti, while the Mysor troops recovered Bahádur Benda. At last a treaty was made (A.D. 1787) by which Bádámi, Kittur, and Nargund were ceded to the Maráthás, who agreed to restore to Tipu the other towns and districts taken by them. Tipu also agreed to pay a tribute and to restore to the nawáb of Sávanur such territory as the latter possessed prior to his son's marriage with Haidar's daughter. The nawáb, however, did not care to trust himself to the tender mercies of his relative by marriage, and accompanied the Maráthás to Poona.[2]

Treaty, A.D. 1787.

Broken by Tipu.

Tipu had seemed anxious to conclude this treaty and had submitted to hard terms, apparently with the determination not to be bound by them, for no sooner had Hari Pant crossed the Krishna than the Mysor troops re-took Kittur. This conduct made the Maráthás eager to make common cause with the other states that had suffered by Tipu's violence and perfidy; and in A.D. 1789 an offensive alliance against him was concluded between the English, the Nizám, and the Peshwa. The Marátha force was placed under the charge of Parsharám Bháu Patvardhan, who went to his jáhgir at Tásgaon to make arrangements. He was joined here by two British battalions under Captain Little, which had landed at Sangameshvar and marched up the Amba pass; and after some vexatious delay the combined English and Marátha force crossed the Krishna. As they proceeded they had little difficulty in expelling Tipu's soldiery, but their progress was checked when they arrived before Dhárwár, the garrison of which had been reinforced. The siege began on the 18th of September, and the British portion of the force soon attacked and took the town, but little further progress was made. The English had no battering train, and the Marátha artillery was poor, badly served, and ill-supplied with ammunition. The besieging force was reinforced by a battalion of Europeans and a native corps under Lieutenant-Colonel Frederick, but as no additional artillery was sent the siege languished, until, at last, a lodgment having been effected by the English and Maráthás

Combined English and Marátha Force, A.D. 1789.

---

[1] It seems to have been retaken immediately. Wilks' Mysor, II. 112.

[2] Grant Duff's Maráthás, III. 12, 13; Wilks' Mysor, II. 117.

HISTORICAL SKETCH, A.D. 1300-1818.

Dhárwár Taken, A.D. 1790.

on the crest of the glacis, the garrison capitulated on the 4th of April 1790. Shortly afterwards Kopál was taken by the Nizám's troops; Kushgal and other places also fell into the hands of the confederates, so that the whole of the Southern Marátha Country was taken from Tipu. By the treaty made at Saringapatan in 1792 the Maráthás were confirmed in their possession of this territory, and Dhondo Pant Gokhalé was made sar-subhedár of the southern portion, most of the districts however falling into the hands of Parsharám Bháu, who had been obliged to raise troops largely in excess of the number for which the Patvardhans' *saranjám* had been assigned.

Disturbances, A.D. 1795-1800.

The Southern Marátha Country was henceforward free from the incursions of Tipu, but the suicide of the Peshwa in 1795 gave rise to a series of intrigues which led to its peace being not a little disturbed. Nána Phadnavis, having broken with the Patvardhan family, incited the rája of Kolhápur to attack their possessions. This the rája did with great effect, and then turned his arms towards the Karnátak which he laid under contribution, repeatedly defeating Dhondo Pant Gokhalé, taking all the strong places between the Ghatprabha and Malprabha rivers, and levying tribute as far south as Kittur. The Kolhápur forces were on one occasion defeated by the sar-subhedár near Sávanur, but on being reinforced recovered their lost ground.[1] The rája's hold of the country however was but short-lived. Parsharám Bháu, having been reconciled to Nána, was sent with the force which it had been intended to employ in the campaign of A.D. 1799 against Tipu to recover the lost territory, and the rája was obliged to retire to Panhála, leaving his capital to be besieged. The death of Nána Phadnavis at this juncture caused new disturbances. Sindia was incited by the new Peshwa Báji Ráo to attack the Patvardhans' jáhgir, and was joined by the Nipáni chief, who wasted the whole country between Miraj and Bijápur.

Dhundia Wágh, A.D. 1790-1800.

Further south, too, there were troubles. On the fall of Saringapatan one Dhundia Wágh, who had been in Tipu's service, managed to make his escape and took service with the rája of Kolhápur. When the latter was besieged, Dhundia set up on his own account as a freebooter, and plundered both the districts which the English had lately acquired from Tipu and those in the south of the Peshwa's dominions. His success drew numerous adherents to his standard, and he assumed the title of King of the Two Worlds. Dhondo Pant Gokhalé, who had been engaged at Kolhápur, returned to the south to put down this formidable marauder, but fell into an ambush and was killed, Chintáman Ráo, the father of the present (1877) chief of Sángli, being wounded on the occasion. Dhundia Wágh did not long enjoy his success. Permission having been granted to the English to follow him into the Peshwa's territory, a force was sent after him under Major-General Wellesley (afterwards the Duke of Wellington), by whom the king of the Two Worlds was followed up vigorously, and at last brought to bay on the 10th of

[1] Stokes' Belgaum, 61.

HISTORICAL SKETCH, A.D. 1300-1818.

September 1800 at Konagal, where he was defeated and killed.[1] The territories wrested from Dhundia Wágh were made over to the Patvardhan family; but as the Peshwa Báji Ráo was determined to ruin that family, Bápu Pant Gokhalé, the nephew and successor of the deceased sar-subhedár, was instructed to throw every obstacle in their way.

Condition of the Southern Marátha Country, A. D. 1803.

The following extract from a letter written by General Wellesley in April 1803[2] gives a succinct but graphic account of the state of the Southern Marátha Country during the two and a half years that had elapsed since the battle of Konagal: "Since the year 1800, when I was in this country before, it has been one continued contest for power and plunder between the different chiefs who have armies under their command; between the Patvardhans (Parsharám Bháu's family) and Gokhalé in the countries bordering on the Tungbhadra Varda and Malprabha; between the Patvardhans and the rája of Kolhápur in those bordering on the Ghatprabha and Krishna; between Bápuji Sindia the killedár of Dhárwár and the rája of Kittur; between Gokhalé and the rája of Kittur, and Gokhalé and Bápuji Sindia; besides various others of inferior note either immediately employed under these or for themselves under their protection." When General Wellesley wrote this letter he was passing through the country on his way to Poona to aid the Peshwa, who had lately concluded the treaty of Bassein. During the campaign against Sindia and the Berar rája, the Southern Marátha Country remained pretty quiet, as the English leader had given it to be clearly understood that he would not have his communications with the south disturbed, and on one occasion ordered up Major-General Campbell from Mysor to keep the peace.

The desái of Nipani, the only one of the southern chiefs except Bápu Pant Gokhalé who took part in the campaign under General Wellesley, was rewarded on his return with the title of sar-lashkar and a considerable saranjám. He devoted a good deal of his attention to fights with Kolhápur and Sávantvádi, which are noted in the account of Kolhápur.

The other chiefs in the south though not so actively turbulent as the Nipáni chief, maintained an attitude of semi-independence of the Peshwa, who was bent on their ruin. Had it not been for the British resident at Poona and the subsidiary force under his orders, doubtless an internecine war would have broken out. Independently of the distrust which Báji Ráo's character and known aims excited, the power placed in the hand of the notorious Trimbakji Denglé caused general disgust. The temper of the country was shown by the refusal of the commandant of Dhárwár to give up that fort to the favourite in accordance with the orders of the Peshwa, who had to send a force to invest the place.[3]

---

[1] Detailed accounts are given in the Wellington Despatches. In Gleig's Life of Sir T. Munro (page 133 of the Condensed Edition) a letter from General Wellesley to Munro is printed, giving a succinct account of the operations against Dhundia Wágh.

[2] Quoted in Stokes' Belgaum, 69.

[3] Grant Duff's Maráthás, 255.

HISTORICAL SKETCH, A.D. 1300-1818.

Dhárwár Ceded to the British, A.D. 1817.

The end of the Peshwa's "robber-government"[1] was at hand. By the treaty of Poona, made in June 1817, he agreed to cede to the English territory in lieu of the contingent he was bound by the treaty of Bassein to maintain; and Dhárwár and Kushgal, together with the districts south of the Varda, were among the cessions. Colonel T. Munro was appointed Commissioner of the ceded districts and made Dhárwár his head-quarters. He was there when the war with the Peshwa broke out at the end of 1817, and thence he started to perform one of the most amazing exploits that have ever been performed, even in India. With five companies of regulars and two field-pieces he calmly proceeded to wrest the Southern Marátha Country from the Peshwa, and to settle it as he went on. Having augmented his scanty force with some *sibandi* or revenue messengers, he began by raising the siege of Navalgund near Dhárwár, which enabled him to get some more troops and a small battering train from the south; after which he took the various strong places in the vicinity of Dhárwár and garrisoned them with peons. He then moved north, taking Bádámi and Bágálkot, and advanced to Gokák. After the battle of Koregaon Báji Ráo had fled to this place with the intention of invading the ceded districts and opening communications with the rája of Mysor.[2] He found that Munro's exertions, popularity, and skilful military arrangements had rendered an attack on the country south of the Ghatprabha hopeless and was forced to retrace his steps. From Gokák, Munro, who had been made Brigadier-General when the war broke out, marched south to Belgaum, where he arrived on the 14th of March 1818. Owing to the smallness of his force and the inefficiency of his battering train,[3] the garison felt themselves secure; and after the siege began, on the 22nd of March, various accidents to the besiegers, the blowing up of a magazine and the bursting of a gun, seemed to render the latter's chances of success even less than before. The besieged however soon found, to their dismay, that notwithstanding all obstacles the enemy made rapid progress; and on the 9th of April the garrison sent out a flag of truce to propose terms, which were refused. The siege went on, a practicable breach was made, and on the 11th of April the garrison gave up the fort and marched out with their arms and private property.[4] After resting a few days General Munro advanced towards Bijápur. As he advanced, to use the words of the historian of the Maráthás, he sent his irregulars to the right and left of his column of march, who occupied the villages, fought with spirit on several occasions, stormed fortified places, and took possession in the name of "Thomas Munro Bahádur." The Peshwa's troops in the vicinity retreated as Munro advanced, and finally took refuge in the

Munro Settles the Southern Maratha Country, A.D. 1817.

Takes Bádámi and Bágalkot, A.D. 1817;

Belgaum, A.D. 1818.

---

[1] General Wellesley in a letter to Colonel Close, the resident at Poona, declared that the Peshwa's "only system of government was that of a robber."

[2] See Prinsep's Transactions in India, 1813-1823, II. 168.

[3] The force consisted of three troops of British dragoons, three artillerymen, eleven companies of Native infantry, four companies of Mysor infantry, and the same number of pioneers. The battering train was composed of one 8-inch mortar, one 5½-inch howitzer, two iron 18-pounders, two iron 12 pounders, and four brass 12-pounders.

[4] In Stokes' Belgaum, 74-77, will be found a more detailed account of the siege.

HISTORICAL SKETCH, A.D. 1300-1818.

fort of Sholápur. The capture of the fortress formed a fitting close to Munro's campaign and completed the conquest of the Southern Marátha Country.

Southern Marátha Country Annexed, A.D. 1818.

By the proclamation issued at Sátára on the 10th of February 1818 annexing to the British dominions the territories of the Peshwa, with certain specified exceptions, the tract of country in question had become British territory. As soon as military operations ceased it was placed in charge of Mr. Chaplin, a Madras Civil Servant, who was appointed, under Mr. Mountstuart Elphinstone, principal Collector of the Marátha Country south of the Krishna and Political Agent with the Rája of Kolhápur and the Southern jághirdárs. The intention of Government at the time was that the Southern Marátha Country should eventually form part of the Madras Presidency; but it was finally decided by the Court of Directors that it should continue to form part of the territory subject to the Government of Bombay.

The history of Sávanur the only state of importance in the Southern Marátha districts may with advantage be separately summarised.

SÁVANUR. Sávanur Nawábs, A.D. 1630.

The Nawábs of Sávanur are by origin Patháns of the Miána tribe. One of their ancestors is said to have entered Hindustán with Timúr's army (A.D. 1300). His descendants seem to have enjoyed some position at the court of Delhi.[1] Bahlol Khán, the founder of the family in the Dakhan, entered the service of Murtaza Nizám Sháh, king of Ahmadnagar, whence he passed into that of Muhammad Ádil Sháh of Bijápur (A.D. 1626-1656). His son Abdul Rahim appears to have done good service under Áli Ádil Sháh II.; but the most distinguished member of the family was Abdul Rahim's son, Abdul Karim, who, by his marriage with the daughter of Masáud Khán, jáhgirdár of Adoni, gained as his wife's dowry the fort of Bágalkot, and, what was of still greater value, the support of the Abyssinian faction at the court, of which his father-in-law was the head. On several occasions Abdul Karim commanded the Bijápur armies during campaigns against the Maráthás, and sometimes with success. On the death of Ali Ádil Sháh in A.D. 1672, Abdul Karim Khán was named for the governorship of the Southern Marátha Country and other territory, but owing to the jealousy of the regent, Khawás Khán, he was not allowed to take up the appointment. On the assassination of the regent Abdul Karim succeeded to supreme power, and under his guidance the Mughals, who came to secure the surrender of Bijápur, were repulsed, and had to make a treaty. On the fall of Bijápur in A.D. 1686, Abdul Ráuf Khán, then the representative of the family, entered the service of the emperor, receiving the title of Diler Khán Bahádur Diler Jang, and an assignment of the twenty-two máháls of Bankápur, Azamnagar

Ancestor takes service in Bijápur, A.D. 1630-1640.

Abdul Ráuf Khán enters Aurangzíb's Service, A.D. 1686.

---

[1] In the account of the family by Mr. (now Sir W.) Elliot, printed in the Memoir of the States of the Southern Marátha Country by Captain West (Selections from Bombay Government Records, New Series, CXIII. 205), the title of nawáb is said to have been assumed at Delhi. It does not seem to have been recognized at Bijápur.

HISTORICAL SKETCH, A.D. 1300-1818.

SÁVANUR.

Abdul Ráuf Khán Founds Sávanur, A.D. 1700.

that is Belgaum, and Torgal. At first he made Bankápur his head-quarters, but afterwards taking a fancy to the site of a small village named Janmaranhalli, he there founded the town of Sávanur or Shráwanur, as the place is called to this day by the Kánarese, probably, it has been suggested, from the new town having been begun in the month of Shráwan.[1] Abdul Ráuf Khán at first acted directly under the emperor and then under the imperial viceroy the Nizám. He did good service in reducing the various half-independent desáis and his son Abdul Gháfar Khán followed the same course. Though the latter met with some checks he must have been generally successful, as at his death nearly the whole of the country between the Krishna and Tungbhadra was subject to him.

Majid Khán Succeeds.

His successor Majid Khán was less fortunate. He began by incurring the hostility of the Nizám by neglecting to apply to the latter for investiture on his succession. The consequence was that a Mughal force marched against Sávanur and the nawáb had to submit. The next treaty was with the Peshwa, in A.D. 1747, to whom Majid Khán had to yield the whole of the country comprised in the present tálukás of Bágalkot, Bádámi, Pádshápur, Kittur, Dhárwár, Navalgund, Parasgad, Dambal, and others, thirty-six in all, and was permitted to retain Mishrikot, Hubli, Bankápur, Hángal, part of Kod and Ránebennur, and Kundgol, in all twenty-two districts. Besides these the nawáb retained the forts of Bankápur, Torgal, and Belgaum; and he seems to have had other territory south of the present Dhárwár collectorate.

Cessions to the Peshwa, A.D. 1747.

Killed in Action, A.D. 1751.

Majid Khán, in concert with the other Pathán nawábs of Kaddapa and Karnul, took a prominent part in the contests between the rival candidates for the Nizám's throne. He intrigued with the French; and in pursuance of a conspiracy in favour of Muzaffar Jang held aloof from Násir Jang, with whose army he was serving on the occasion when the latter met his death. He afterwards conspired against Muzaffar Jang and was killed in the action in which the latter also met with the same fate (A.D. 1751).[2]

Abdul Hakim Khán Succeeds, A.D. 1751.

His son Abdul Hakim Khán had not long succeeded when he had to face a formidable confederation and to give up much of his possessions. He imprudently received into his service an officer who had first been in that of the Nizám and then in that of the Peshwa, and when the surrender of the man was demanded by the Peshwa the nawáb refused to comply with the request. He had incurred the enmity also of the Nizám Salábat Jang, whose supremacy he had declined to acknowledge; so the two princes combined against him. An army under Báláji Báji Ráo marched against Sávanur and was joined there by a force under the famous French leader Bussy, with a splendid train of artillery. The nawáb was assisted by the well-known Morári Ráo of Guti, but the besieging force was too strong for him and he had to submit to a treaty

Besieged by the Nizám and Peshwa, A.D. 1756.

[1] Memoir of the States of the Southern Marátha Country, 207.

[2] Malleson's History of the French in India, 251, 263, and 272-73.

(A.D. 1756), by which he agreed to pay eleven lákhs in cash and to cede to the Peshwa the districts of Mishrikót, Hubli, and Kundgol, receiving in compensation part of Ránebennur and Parasgad. The estimated revenue of the districts left in the nawáb's possession was nearly eight lákhs of rupees yearly.

Attacked by Haidar Ali, A.D. 1764.

The connection of Sávanur and the Nizám seems to have ceased from this date, and the nawáb henceforward had to deal only with the Maráthás and with Haidar Ali and his son Tipu. Abdul Hakim Khán was first brought into contact with the Mysor princes in 1764, when Haidar endeavoured to induce him to turn against the Maráthás, and on his refusal attacked and defeated him. The invasion was repelled by the Peshwa in the following year, and Haidar was obliged to give up all claims on Sávanur. He soon renewed his attacks, and succeeded in getting possession of the country between the Krishna and Tungbhadra. Instead of crushing the nawáb he entered into a negotiation with him which ended in a double marriage, the eldest son of Abdul Hakim Khan being married to Haidar's daughter, the most notorious scold in the South of India according to Colonel Wilks, while the nawáb's daughter was married to Haidar's second son Karim Sáheb. The double wedding was celebrated with great magnificence at Saringapatan; and such of the nawáb's possessions as had been taken from him by Haidar were restored, the tribute of four lákhs that had been imposed being, at the same time, reduced by one-half, on condition of a contingent of 2000 horse being maintained for Haidar's service.[1]

Connection by Marriage with Haidar.

Sávanur taken by Tipu,

On the death of Haidar, Tipu took offence at the nawáb's neglect in not sending messages of condolence, and made a demand for a large sum of money, on the ground that the contingent had not been properly maintained. Abdul Hakim Khán applied to the Maráthás for aid, which was granted. In the course of the hostilities that ensued Sávanur was taken by Tipu, and all the nawáb's property seized and destroyed. By the treaty that was subsequently made Tipu agreed to restore to the nawáb such territory as the latter had possessed prior to his son's marriage with Haidar's daughter, but the nawáb did not venture to remain at Sávanur, and went to Poona, where he subsisted on a monthly pension of £1000 (Rs. 10,000) allowed him by the Maráthás. By the treaty of Saringapatan all the territory north of the Tungbhadra was ceded to the Peshwa, and Sávanur seems to have been practically annexed. Abdul Hakim Khán died in A.D. 1795, and his adopted son Abdul Kheir Khán returned to Sávanur, while Hussain Mia, his second son, succeeded to the allowance.[2] When General Wellesley, after the fall of Saringapatan, marched through the country he found the family in great distress, as they had no territorial possessions and their allowance was most irregularly paid. By the General's influence the pension was commuted, and the revenue of twenty-five villages, assessed at £4800 (Rs. 48,000) a year was assigned

Practically annexed by the Peshwa.

Assignment of Twenty-five Villages.

[1] Wilks' Mysor (Indian Reprint), I. 417.

[2] The eldest son, Tipu's brother-in-law, had gone to Saringapatan some years before It does not appear that he ever returned.

HISTORICAL SKETCH, A.D. 1300-1818. *SÁVANUR.*

to the nawáb. This arrangement was afterwards continued by the British Government. At first the nawáb was not allowed to exercise jurisdiction, but afterwards his name was entered in the list of first class sardárs, and he was allowed to exercise certain powers. Full powers were allowed to Nawáb Abdul Dalél Khán, who, in 1862, was made a member of the Bombay Legislative Council. On his death in the same year, Abdul Kheir Khán succeeded. He died in 1868, leaving a son, Abdul Dalél Khán, then six years of age, who was installed as his successor, and who is at present (1877) being educated under the superintendence of the Collector and Political Agent at Dhárwár.

LAPSED STATES.

LAPSED STATES.

In the foregoing sketch it has been mentioned how certain states forming part of the great Patvardhan grants lapsed to the British owing to the last holders' death without heirs. The following statement gives the chief details of these lapses:

LAPSED STATES.

STATE.	Lapse.	Estimated Revenue at time of Lapse.	Brought under the Regulations by
	A.D.	Rs.	
1. Chinchni	1836	1,82,979	Act VIII. of 1839.
2. Gopál Ráo's Share in the Miraj State...	1842	77,658	Bombay Act III. of 1863.
3. Váman Ráv Sonikar's Share in ditto.	1845	85,850	Ditto.
4. Tásgaon	1848	1,76,000	Ditto.
5. Sherbál or Kágvád.	1857	1,12,000	Ditto.
6. Nargund	1858	49,363	Ditto.

The lands comprised in these states now form part of the collectorates of Sátára, Sholápur, Belgaum, and Dhárwár.

The forfeiture of the Nargund state for the treason of the last chief has also been noted. It did not, however, come within the scope of that sketch to give any account of the states of Kittur and Nipáni, which also lapsed under circumstances which will now be narrated.

Kittur.

The Kittur state was held by Lingáyat desáis. The founders of the family are said to have been two brothers, both bearing the name of Malla, to which one prefixed the epithet Hiré or elder, and the other that of Chikka or younger. They were originally merchants, but are said to have distinguished themselves in the Bijápur army; and eventually the family obtained a grant from the Bijápur kings of the sar deshmukhi of the Hubli district, after which they settled at Kittur. On the fall of Bijápur the Kittur desáis became vassals of the Sávanur nawáb, and when the power of that chief was circumscribed they became tributaries to the Peshwa. Kittur suffered much during the campaigns between Mysor and the Maráthás, and for a time had to transfer its allegiance to the former power. Tipu

HISTORICAL SKETCH, A.D. 1300-1818.

LAPSED STATES.

Kittur Taken by Tipu.

twice took the place, and on one of these occasions carried off the desái Mallapa. Mallápa made his escape and joined the Maráthás, who recovered his territory but appropriated it to themselves, putting the desái on an allowance. During the confusion consequent on the death of the Peshwa Mahádév Ráo, the desai managed to drive out the Marátha mámlatdár and resume possession; subsequently, in the war of 1803, he assisted General Wellesley with a small contingent and thereby obtained the powerful mediation of the latter, who brought about a settlement of his affairs. In 1809 the desái succeeded in obtaining a sanad from the Peshwa confirming him in possession of the táluka of Kittur, on condition of the yearly payment of £17,500 (Rs. 1,75,000) and of maintaining a contingent. There is little doubt that this grant would have been ere long resumed had it not been for the fall of the Peshwa not many years after. When the war with Báji Ráo broke out the desái showed himself well disposed towards the English, and was confirmed in the possession of his state on favourable terms by General Munro.

The Desái gets a Sanad from the Peshwa, A.D. 1809.

Confirmed by General Munro, A.D. 1817.

Fictitious Adoption, A.D. 1824.

In September 1824 Mr. Thackeray, the principal Collector, received a letter at Dhárwár purporting to be from the desái, and dated the 10th July, in which the adoption of a son was announced, the servant who brought the letter stating, at the same time, that his master was dying. The civil surgeon was immediately sent to Kittur and found that the desái had been dead several hours. No application for permission to adopt had previously been made, and when Mr. Thackeray had last seen the desái the latter had never expressed any wish to adopt. The signature of the letter, also, was not like the desái's handwriting. These suspicious circumstances led to an enquiry by which it was ascertained that the desái had actually died without making an adoption, and that his kárbháris had invested a child with the insignia, and had put a pen in the dead man's hand with which they signed the letter announcing the adoption. It was further ascertained that no descendant of the desái who held the state before its conquest by Tipu was alive, and that no near connection of the deceased desái, in the female line, was to be found. The boy alleged to have been adopted was, if connected with the family at all, descended from a collateral branch so remote that its descent from the common ancestor could not be traced.

Revolt of Kittur.

While the question as to the course to be adopted was under consideration by Government, Mr. Thackeray found it necessary to take steps for the security of the state treasury, and proceeded to Kittur accompanied by a troop of golandáz. He at first attempted persuasion; but finding that there were signs of an approaching outbreak he considered it advisable to take two guns into the outer fort, which were posted at the gateways. The next morning (the 23rd of October) the gates were found locked and the inner fort full of armed men. Preparations were being made, after milder measures had failed, to blow open the gate with the other two guns, when a sudden sally was made from the fort, and three officers who were with the guns were cut down. Mr. Thackeray, who came up at this juncture, was shot and cut to pieces, and his assistants, Messrs. Stevenson and Elliot[1]

Mr. Thackeray Killed.

[1] The late Sir Walter Elliot, K.C.S.I.

HISTORICAL SKETCH, A.D. 1300-1818.

LAPSED STATES. Revolt of Kittur, 1824.

were taken into the fort as prisoners. It was some time before a force could be assembled sufficiently strong to capture Kittur, and it was not till the 30th of November that the fort was invested. The insurgents attempted to obtain terms, but were referred to the proclam a tion that had been issued by Government, and were warned of the terrible punishment that would follow if any harm was done to the prisoners. At last, on the 2nd of December, Messrs. Stevenson and Elliot were released; but as the fort was not given up, it was attacked, and a practicable breach having been made, it was surrendered on the 4th of December 1824 by the garrison.

Fort Taken.

State Lapses.

The yearly revenue of the Kittur state that thus lapsed to Government was £33,365 (Rs. 3,33,647) exclusive of alienations amounting to upwards of £4000 (Rs. 40,000) more. The territory was brought under the regulations by Regulation VII. of 1830, and now forms part of the collectorates of Dhárwár and Belgaum.

Nipáni.

The Nipáni state is of recent origin. The chief was a desái who distinguished himself in the Peshwa's service. In the campaign against Sindia and the Berar rája in 1803, he accompanied General Wellesley as commandant of a contingent of the Peshwa's troops. For the good service he did on this and other occasions he was rewarded by Báji Ráo with the title of Sar-Lashkar and with the grant of a very considerable saranjam. During the war of 1817 Sidoji Ráo sar-lashkar joined the Peshwa late, and never acted cordially against the British. He was accordingly, on the dethronement of Báji Ráv, confirmed in the possession of his saranjam.

Supposititious Heir, A.D. 1831.

The Nipáni chief, though he had six wives, had no son. As there was no genuine heir it was determined to introduce a supposititious one, and accordingly in 1831, Tái Bái, one of the chief's wives, left the fort and went to reside in a house in the town, giving out that she was with child and wished to be delivered there. A widow, who was really in this condition, was introduced into the house and there gave birth to a male child which was immediately passed off by Tái Bái as her son, the unfortunate mother being made away with for fear of her subsequently claiming the child or divulging the imposture. These facts were brought to the notice of Government, which, taking into consideration the chief's age and former services, waived their right to resume the saranjám at once, but informed him that in consequence of the fraud that had been proved against him the saranjám would lapse on his death whether he left male heirs or not. Accordingly, on the death of the chief in 1839, the saranjámi estate was at once resumed[1] and the districts and villages composing it were divided between the collectorates of Dhárwár Belgaum and Sholápur. The net revenue was estimated at £18,369 (Rs. 1,83,690) but much of the land was waste, so that the revenue under proper management would have been far larger. The territory was brought under the regulations by Act VI. of 1842.

Saranjám Lapses, A.D. 1839.

---

[1] The deshgat property passed to the adopted son of the late chief.